Citizen Demand-Making
in the Urban Context

Citizen Demand-Making in the Urban Context

Elaine B. Sharp

The University of Alabama Press

Copyright © 1986 by
The University of Alabama Press
University, Alabama 35486
All rights reserved
Manufactured in the United States of America

Library of Congress Cataloging in Publication Data

Sharp, Elaine B.
  Citizen demand-making in the urban context.

  Bibliography: p.
  Includes index.
  1. Kansas City (Mo.)—Politics and government.
2. Citizens' associations—Missouri—Kansas City.
3. Municipal government—United States—Case studies.
4. Political participation—Missouri—Kansas City.
I. Title.
JS982.S5   1986   352.0778'411   85-8536
ISBN 0-8173-0275-1 (alk. paper)

One may say that these are petty affairs, but they are not petty to those whom they immediately touch. And, anyway, most of life, individual and collective, consists of petty affairs.

—Walter Gellhorn,
When Americans Complain

Contents

Tables and Figures	ix
Acknowledgments	xi
1. Citizen-Initiated Contacts as Urban Demand-Making	1
2. Patterns of Contacting: The Socioeconomic and the Need-Awareness Models	32
3. The Neighborhood Context for Demand-Making	57
4. What Difference Does a Central Complaints Unit Make?	102
5. Demand-Making and Mobility: Tiebout Revisited	133
6. Urban Governance and Demand Overload	162
Appendix: Citizen Survey Methodology	186
References	202
Index	210

Tables and Figures

Tables

2-1	Socioeconomic Characteristics of Persons Who Had Contacted a City Official in the Last Year	33
2-2	Race of Persons Who Had Contacted a City Official in the Last Year	33
2-3	Relationships between Socioeconomic Variables and Various Forms of Contacting Behavior	37
2-4	Contacting and Political Awareness	41
2-5	Socioeconomic Status and Political Awareness	41
2-6	Socioeconomic Variables and Six Types of Political Participation	44
2-7	Perceived Need and Contacting	50
2-8	Explaining Contacting: Multiple Regression Results	55
3-1	Perceived Need and Objective Need in the Neighborhood	66
3-2	Objective Need and Contacting	66
3-3	Results of Regression of Perceived Need on Hypothesized Determinants	76
3-4	Associations between Specific Measures of Objective Conditions and Residents' Perceptions of Those Problems	79
3-5	Need-Awareness Status of the Neighborhood and Contacting Propensity	86
4-1	Targets of Citizen-Initiated Contacts	103
4-2	Targets of Citizen-Initiated Contacts, by Education	104
4-3	Targets of Citizen-Initiated Contacts, by Race	104
4-4	Evaluations of Government Response to Contact by Target of Contact	115
4-5	Perceptions of Government Responsiveness (I) by Ratings of How Well Contact Was Handled	120
4-6	Perceptions of Government Responsiveness (II) by Ratings of How Well Contact Was Handled	121

4-7 Perceptions of Government Responsiveness by Evaluation of How Contact Was Handled (Action Center Debriefees)	126
5-1 Moving Plans of a 1978 National Sample	146
5-2 Reasons for Selecting Present Location, 1978 National Sample	149
5-3 Most Important Reason for Selecting Present Location, 1978 National Sample	151
5-4 The Decision to Move under Various Hypothetical Circumstances	152
5-5 Mobility and Political Participation	157
5-6 Mobility and Evaluations of Government's Response to Contact	158
5-7 Mobility and Perceptions of Government Responsiveness	159

Figures

1-1 The Socioeconomic Model	9
1-2 The Need-Awareness Model	13
1-3 A Synthetic Model of Contacting Propensity	16
1-4 Selection Matrix for the Study Neighborhoods	28
1-5 Kansas City Study Neighborhoods	30
2-1 Education and Contacting	47
2-2 Income and Contacting	47
2-3 The Need-Awareness Model: Possible Scenarios	48
2-4 Average Need and Knowledge Levels, by Education Group	53
3-1 Education, Contacting, and the Neighborhood Socioeconomic Context	61
3-2 Objective Need, Expectations, and Perceived Need: Hypotheses	69
3-3 Objective Need, Expectations, and Perceived Need: Results	75
3-4 Need, Awareness, and Contacting Propensity: 24 Kansas City Study Neighborhoods	85
4-1 Propensity to Contact the Action Center by Neighborhood Social Well-Being	111
4-2 Contacts with Officials Other than the Action Center, by Neighborhood Social Well-Being	112

Acknowledgments

This book is the end product of a project to which many individuals contributed in various ways. I owe special thanks to Michael Eggleston and Rick Feiock for their efforts in the data-collection phase and to the programming staff at the Center for Public Affairs for their help with everything from data entry to laser printing. Dwight Kiel provided very helpful comments to clarify a point in the discussion that seemed to be hopelessly entangled. The project would not have been possible were it not for the cooperation of many Kansas Citians, especially those community leaders who graciously gave of their time for interviews and officials in the City Development Department and the Action Center who were helpful in numerous ways. I acknowledge with gratitude that the project was supported by the National Science Foundation under Grant No. SES-8200435. Any opinions, findings, conclusions, or recommendations expressed here are my own, however, and do not necessarily reflect the views of the National Science Foundation.

Figure 1-2 is adapted from Bryan Jones, Saadia Greenberg, Joseph Kaufman, and Joseph Drew, "Bureaucratic Response to Citizen Initiated Contacts: Environmental Enforcement in Detroit," *American Political Science Review* 72 (1977), by permission of the American Political Science Association.

Figures 2-1 and 2-2 and parts of Chapters 2 and 6 are from Elaine B. Sharp, "Citizen Demand-Making in the Urban Context," *American Journal of Political Science* 28 (November 1984), by permission of the publisher, the University of Texas Press, Austin.

Figure 4-1 and parts of Chapter 4 are from Elaine B. Sharp, "Need Awareness, and Contacting Propensity: Study of a City with a Central Complaints Unit," *Urban Affairs Quarterly* 20 (September 1984), by permission of the publisher, Sage Publications, Beverly Hills.

Chapter 5 was given as a paper, "Local Government Services and Residential Mobility," at the Annual Meetings of the American Political Science Association, Washington, D.C., September 1984, copyright by the American Political Science Association.

Parts of Chapter 3 were given in "The Roots of Urban Demand-Making," a paper presented at the Annual Meetings of the Midwest Political Science Association, Chicago, April 1984.

1

Citizen-Initiated Contacts as Urban Demand-Making

Cities, like most complex entities, can be analyzed from a variety of perspectives. The city has been treated from an ecological standpoint as a "human aggregation living in a fixed, geographical locale and controlled by the subcultural processes of competition, cooperation, assimilation, and conflict" (Reissman, 1970: 103). The city has also been viewed as a place of citizenship and community or as a fortress in which the underclass of society is trapped (Long, 1972). It has also been seen as a spatial configuration of "processes of class conflict and capital accumulation" (Gottdiener, 1983: 231) or as a system of "trenches" through which labor is aggregated yet kept distinct from residential political groupings (Katznelson, 1981). The city has even, from a Freudian perspective, been treated as an exemplar of the ways in which "'civilization' alienated the 'natural personality' from basic instinctual needs and drives" (Smith, 1979: 50).

One of the most powerful contemporary treatments, however, focuses on city government and likens it to a firm, providing an array of services to citizen-consumers. This approach may be traced to Charles Tiebout's (1956) classic exposition of the metropolitan area as a marketplace of local governments, each providing a characteristic package of services and taxes and competing for citizen-consumers. However debatable Tiebout's thesis may be, interpretations of the city as a service-providing entity are by now firmly entrenched. Indeed, the study of urban politics in recent years has increasingly focused on delivery of urban services (Lineberry, 1977; Levy, Meltsner, and Wildavsky, 1974;

Rich, 1982a). Alternative institutional arrangements for effective and equitable distribution of urban services have been extensively studied (Bish and Ostrom, 1973; Frederickson, 1973; Washnis, 1972; Ostrom, 1976; Rich, 1982b), and special attention is now being given to the ways in which the supply of services by government producers compares with the supply by private producers (Savas, 1982).

A service-production model of the city must, of course, include attention to the demand as well as the supply side of public services. Because most urban public services are not "marketed," however, the strict, economics meaning of "demand" is inappropriate. In urban politics, demand does not necessarily reflect a willingness to pay, as registered in the volume of services "purchased" at a particular price. Rather, demand refers to the variety of ways in which citizens register their preference for the delivery of a particular service at a particular time and place or for a change in the quality or quantity of service delivered.

Partly because of the structure of urban government and partly because of the distinctive characteristics of urban services, demand-making in the urban setting frequently involves direct, personal contact between citizen-consumers and government producers—particularly the personnel of urban service bureaucracies. Douglas Yates (1977) argues that the fragmentation of urban government, coupled with the "daily, direct, and locality specific" nature of urban services, creates the context for individualistic and personalized demand-making: "Urban service delivery often involves a street-level relationship that is not only direct but personal. Consider the relationship between citizens and city government in police, education, welfare, and health services. In those arenas the character of service delivery is heavily dependent on the attitudes, values, and behavior of the particular citizens and public employees involved" (Yates, 1977: 20).

Furthermore, demand-making in the urban context tends to focus on administrative actors: "Because service delivery lies at the heart of city government and because service delivery involves at root an ongoing service relationship between citizens and street-level bureaucrats, urban policymaking has a distinctively bureaucratic and administrative flavor" (Yates, 1977: 26–27). Recognition of these special features of the "service-delivery" city has been accompanied by interest in a form of demand-making that had been ignored. Peter Eisinger was one of the first to propose its importance: "One means by which individual citizens express policy preferences and communicate grievances directly to public officials, namely personally initiated contacts with government personnel, is a subject which has commanded little attention among social scientists" (1972: 43).

Since Eisinger's observation in 1972, however, interest in citizen-initiated contacting as a form of political behavior and in the institutional arrangements for facilitating such demand-making has increased markedly. These developments are reviewed below. Here it is important to note that the growing interest in citizen-initiated complaints and requests for service, like the larger interest in the politics of urban service delivery of which it is a part, represents a new thrust in the study of urban politics, as well as a new opportunity in the analysis of citizen participation. The study of urban politics has traditionally focused on the local-level equivalent of interest-group politics at the national level, but with a distinctly conflictual flavor reflective of citizen action movements that have emerged in urban areas. Case studies of conflict between neighborhood groups and city government or other major institutions over siting of facilities and major development issues form the nucleus of the literature on urban politics (Meyerson and Banfield, 1955; Banfield, 1961), a pattern that continued with case studies of conflict over the Community Action Program. Citizen demand-making in this literature is embodied in familiar and dramatic forms of participation—political organization, protest activity, and the like.

Citizen-initiated contacting of government officials is a much more routine, invisible activity, geared toward matters of everyday service delivery rather than large-scale policy issues. Citizen contacting of government officials therefore has little of the glamour of case studies of confrontations between city government and citizen groups. Furthermore, at first blush, such contacts may appear to be such low-level, individualistic, nonpolitical acts as hardly to warrant inclusion as a mode of citizen participation along with acts such as voting, campaign activity, and other attempts to influence political representation.

But if the study of politics is the study of "who gets what, when, and how" (Lasswell, 1936), citizen-initiated contacts with government officials are surely a significant element of urban politics. As Eisinger notes: "Citizen contact with people in government is an important dimension of the representation relationship: contact is a demand for representation in that the contactor asks in effect that an official act on behalf of his concerns" (1972: 43).

If urban services were distributed by some criteria other than responsiveness to such individual contacts, their relevance for who gets what would be small. But there is by now considerable evidence that urban service bureaucracies are, by and large, structured to deliver on demand. As Aaron Wildavsky argues, the uncertainties surrounding the urban service bureaucracy drive it toward decision rules that make citizen demands the key to service delivery: "Our bureaucrat deals with this uncertainty by vastly oversimplifying his view of the environment, and by devising operational procedures that greatly decrease the need for information. This bureaucrat accordingly will limit the agency's actions to clients who present actual demands—a small portion of its potential clients. . . . He will rely upon what we call Adam Smith rules: when a customer makes a 'request,' take care of that client in a professional manner; otherwise, leave him alone" (1979: 360).

Clearly, Adam Smith rules are not operational in all urban bureaucracies all of the time. But when a street department schedules repairs based on complaints about potholes, when tree trimming is provided on request by citizens, when a substantial portion of the inspections conducted by building code enforcement personnel are in response to requests, and when police departments dispatch a squad car each time a citizen calls for help with a problem, however minor, we can say that the distribution of the city's public service resources hinges upon citizen-initiated contacts.

Likewise, if all citizens were equally prone to register such demands upon urban government, this topic would have less relevance for understanding urban politics. Citizens are not all equally prone to make demands, however, as Eisinger notes:

> Some citizens make no contacts whatsoever, but among the substantial number who do, the targets and concerns vary widely. Given the variety of contact patterns, it follows that some citizens are represented through the device of contact more than others or differently than others. That some citizens seize this opportunity for representation while others do not and that citizens pursue contacts with different officials . . . make the study of the patterns of contact an enterprise of considerable importance in understanding how and to whom representative political systems respond. [1972: 44]

For the analyst of urban politics, then, citizen-initiated contacting has emerged as a significant form of political behavior. Such demand-making is not of interest to analysts alone, however. As the next section outlines, city governments have also recognized the significance of this form of demand-making and have moved to institutionalize new arrangements for handling citizen-initiated contacts.

Institutional Arrangements for Demand-Making: From Precinct Committeeman to Executive Ombudsman

A variety of choices faces the citizen who wishes to register a complaint with the city or make a request for service delivery. One can write a letter to the mayor, call a city council member, get in touch with the appropriate city department, or ask a neighborhood association to forward one's problem to the city government.

It has often been noted that the era of the urban political machine provided citizens with a clear contact point for access to city hall: "It is well known that the great machines provided personal services to immigrants needing assistance and mediation in dealing with a distant and unfamiliar government. This is the classic machine role vividly depicted by George Washington Plunkett, the shoestand philosopher of Tammany Hall" (Yates, 1977: 45). Citizen-initiated contacting, in such a milieu, need involve nothing more than a close relationship with one's precinct captain.

The reform movement that changed the face of urban politics in America also had implications for the process of citizen-initiated contacts with government. In particular, the reform movement was accompanied by increasing specialization and professionalization in urban government. The machine politics ethic, under which those tied to the machine have clout in the dispensation of urban services, was to be replaced by neutral, professional administration—or, as Victor Thompson (1975) aptly describes it, administration "without sympathy or enthusiasm." To the extent that delivery of urban services has become increasingly professionalized and removed from partisan politics, old modes of connection to city hall via ward and precinct leaders have become less relevant.

But the passing of the machine politics era is by no means the only, or even the primary, reason for the development of new mechanisms for citizens to contact city hall. The increasing complexity of the service-delivery city is also a factor. As Walter Gellhorn notes:

> Despite the physical immediacy of the citizen's relationship to municipal government, the intimacy of earlier times has been destroyed by the multiplication of tasks assigned to urban officials. In New York City . . . the list of licenses, permits, or certificates that must be obtained from local officials contains 859

topic headings; an owner of a residential property may have dealings with more than a dozen different agencies; the "little green book," a municipally published vest-pocket directory of addresses, officials, and functions, devotes 252 pages to city affairs. [1966: 153]

Eisinger provides an equally graphic description of the problems confronting the citizen who wishes to register a complaint or request:

> Contemplating the task evokes visions of Kafkaesque corridors and frosted glass doors in anonymous buildings. The problems of making contact with bureaucrats often approach the absurd . . . to complain in New York City about the sale of unsanitary food one must telephone the Department of Health. But to notify the proper official that one has become ill from the unsanitary food he bought, the citizen must call a different number at the same department. And if the food is unsanitary because it has remained on the shelf too long, the hapless shopper must call still a third number. [1972: 44]

Partly in response to these problems, and perhaps partly because of the popularity of the ombudsman institution in other countries (Gellhorn, 1966), many American cities have established ombudsmanlike, centralized, complaint-handling offices. Although these offices go by many names, they constitute a peculiarly American or administrative ombudsman approach. Unlike the classic Scandinavian ombudsman, such offices are typically housed organizationally within the administrative structure of city government (as part of the city manager's or mayor's office, for example); and although the ombudsman's office has traditionally been perceived as dealing with the problem of officials who exceed their authority or run roughshod over citizens in some way, the American urban complaint bureau is oriented more toward the problem that "officials had not done what they were supposed to do, rather than that they were doing what they were authorized to do" (Gellhorn, 1966: 65). Finally, unlike the classic ombudsman's office, which typically has investigative powers and functions, these urban complaint bureaus have a more straightforward referral and follow-up function. Kansas City, Missouri—the site for the research reported here—has such a centralized complaint-handling unit. As the following section shows, the existence of this unit introduces an important contingency for analysis of patterns of citizen-initiated contacting because one of the two key explanatory models of contacting propensity may be sensitive to the organizational context in which contacting is studied.

Explaining Patterns of Contact Behavior

Existing research on citizen-initiated contacting revolves around two basic explanatory models: a socioeconomic model and a need-awareness model. The former is based on the assumption that contacting, like many other forms of political participation, should be a positive function of one's socioeconomic status. The possible role of political attitudes and skills as intervening variables is not always made explicit in research based on the socioeconomic model. In the model's fully articulated form, however, political attitudes help to specify why socioeconomic variables such as income and education would be expected to predict levels of political participation. As Norman Nie et al. explain: "The high social status citizen does not *just* participate in politics; he does so only when he has the attitudes such as efficacy and attentiveness which are postulated as intervening variables. Social status, then, affects rates of political participation through its effect on political attitudes . . . it means that intervening attitude variables explain *how* a citizen's social status affects his political activity" (1969: 811). In sum, the socioeconomic model (Figure 1-1), adapted to the case of citizen-initiated contacting, hypothesizes that variables such as income and education should be the paramount predictors of contacting, in large part because higher-income and better-educated individuals are more likely to

FIGURE 1-1. *The Socioeconomic Model*

have political attitudes that predispose them toward political action. Citizen-initiated contacting, according to this model, is another in a spectrum of acts of political participation; and as such, it can be understood according to the conventional model that has long been used to explain differential propensities to participate.

Many, however, have been skeptical of the relevance of the socioeconomic model for contacting on the grounds that contacting is essentially different from other behaviors that have been traditionally treated as acts of political participation. Undeniably, there are substantial differences between contacting and traditional acts of political assertion such as voting, campaign activity, and community group involvement. Philip Coulter aptly summarizes these unique features of citizen-initiated contacting: "Through contacting, a citizen takes the initiative, i.e., chooses the nature, content, referent, target, level of government, and timing of the contact. Contacting is harder than most participatory acts, because the citizen must take the initiative and make the effort. And because the citizen must set the policy agenda of a contact, the subject-matter is automatically important and salient to him/her" (1984: 5–6). Unlike voting, campaign activity, and community organization involvement then, contacting is a direct, individualistic, high-initiative activity. These characteristics, however, would not appear to introduce reservations about the applicability of the socioeconomic model. Indeed, a sense of political efficacy and similar attitudes and skills that the socioeconomic model posits as being more likely among upper-status citizens might be viewed as especially important for a more "difficult" political act such as contacting.

The challenge to the applicability of the socioeconomic model comes, rather, from perspectives on the narrowness and instrumental nature of contacting, or at least contacting in one of its forms. To understand the characterization, it is important to consider the distinction, originated by Sidney Verba and Norman Nie (1972), between "particularized" and "general referent" contacting. According to Verba and Nie, the latter form involves the making of demands on issues of broad significance for the community. Particularized contacts, on the other hand, involve narrower matters—requests or complaints of relevance primarily to the contactors or their family (why *their* trash was not collected or why *their* water meter was misread, for example).

In their factor analysis of national sample survey data, Verba and Nie find that general referent contacting fits nicely into a dimension of communal participation; and communal participation, like other modes of political participation, is well explained by the standard socioeconomic model. Particularized contacting, on the other hand, is a mode of activity that stands distinct from voting, campaigning, and communal participation, and the standard socioeconomic model does not explain variation in it (Verba and Nie, 1972: 136). Further, Verba and Nie find that those who engage in particularized contacting primarily are "parochial participants": "These citizens are lower than any other group—including the inactives—in their sense of contributing to the community, thus underscoring the extent to which their political activity is focused on the narrow problems of their own personal lives. This is paralleled by a low level of psychological involvement, a relative absence of partisanship, and a somewhat lower than average level on the other measures of involvement in conflict and cleavage" (1972: 90–91). These findings have had considerable impact on prevailing conceptions of the nature of citizen-initiated contacting. According to Coulter (1984: 21), their impact may have been buttressed by prevailing biases in the political science discipline, including biases toward the significance of electoral participation, biases concerning the significance of study of national and comparative political phenomena relative to local phenomena, and assumptions that dramatic, ideological, issue-oriented behaviors and events are "superior" to routine, instrumental, administratively oriented behaviors. Coulter (1984) found, in a study conducted in Birmingham, that particularized contactors are not parochial participants. Rather, they show above-average levels of involvement in other forms of political participation. Coulter's (1984) analysis constitutes a revisionist approach in reaction to the outpouring of research on contacting since 1972, much of it influenced by Verba and Nie's (1972) characterization. Of considerable importance in that research was the development of an alternative explanatory model for contacting—a model keyed to the unique, instrumental nature of contacting rather than one keyed to the socioeconomic explanation that Verba and Nie (1972) had presumably discredited for this purpose.

That alternative model is a need-awareness model, developed by Bryan Jones and colleagues (1977). According to this model, socioeconomic variables are not the key to understanding contacting propensity. Rather, contacting is a function of two factors: need for government services and awareness of government. The awareness factor may be construed broadly as incorporating the citizen's recognition that certain services are the responsibility of city government and the citizen's level of political sophistication about means of obtaining access to city government with regard to those services. The awareness component provides a bridge between this new explanatory model and the standard socioeconomic model because the political information and skills that the awareness dimension encompasses are similar to the political predispositions and skills that serve as intervening variables in the socioeconomic model.

What is most unique about this alternative model is the need component. As Jones and colleagues note: "One of the curious omissions of the classic literature on participation is any discussion of the individual's need for the policies or services" (1977: 150). They speculate that need has been overlooked because the most-studied forms of participation—campaigning and voting—do not appear to be need-based and because the success of the socioeconomic model in explaining such forms of participation obviates any attention to need. The instrumental character of contacting, however, invites attention to need as an explanatory factor.

The need-awareness model stipulates that sufficient levels of *both* need and awareness are necessary before citizens are predisposed to contact city government. Since the need-awareness model is designed to account for differences in contacting propensity across neighborhoods, neighborhood "social well-being" serves roughly as a neighborhood-level equivalent of socioeconomic status. Need is posited to be inversely associated with social well-being, and awareness is presumed to be positively associated with social well-being. Therefore, the need-awareness model predicts that contacting propensity should be highest in neighborhoods at the middle of the social well-being range (see Figure 1-2). In better-off areas, political awareness is at a high level, but there is little need for attention from government; in worse-off areas, there is much need but little political awareness.

Empirical research on patterns of contacting has not provided conclusive evidence about the relative merits of the socioeconomic and the need-awareness models. Instead, contradictory findings have proliferated. In a study of contacting in Garland, Texas, for example, Arnold Vedlitz and Eric Veblen (1980) found evidence for the socioeconomic model rather than the need-awareness model. Another study of contacting, in Wichita, Kansas, also showed support for the socioeconomic model rather than the need-awareness model (Sharp, 1982). Neither of these is consistent with Verba and Nie's (1972) analysis, which found no association between socioeconomic status variables and particularized contacts. Meanwhile, Vedlitz, James Dyer, and Roger Durand (1980) found negative, linear relationships between social well-being and contacting propensity in Dallas and Houston—results inconsistent with both the socioeconomic and the need-awareness models.

There are a variety of possible explanations for these contradictory findings. One is the "cities are all different" explanation. The empirical research reviewed above was conducted in a variety of cities, ranging from Wichita to Dallas to Detroit to Garland,

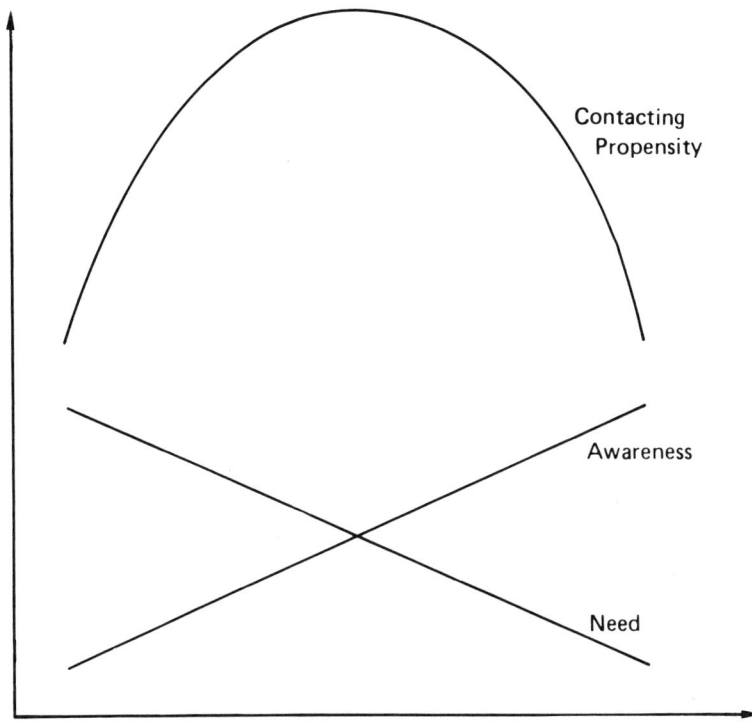

FIGURE 1-2. *The Need-Awareness Model*

Texas. At a superficial level, one might simply conclude that there is no universal model of contacting and that patterns of contacting differ, for unspecified reasons, from city to city. Better still, Vedlitz and Veblen (1980) suggest a particular reason for differences in contacting patterns across cities—that a key factor may be whether a city has a centralized complaint-handling unit. In cities that do not, political awareness may be inversely associated with social status, as the need-awareness model stipulates. The introduction of a centralized complaint-handling unit might be expected to level out differences in political awareness, however, thus making need a more important explanatory factor.

The contradictory empirical findings reviewed above might

also be the result of important differences in study designs. Some studies, most notably the Detroit study, which generated the need-awareness model (Jones et al., 1977), are based on analysis of citizen contacts recorded by the city bureaucracy, aggregated to some areal unit of analysis. Other studies, including both of those that found support for the socioeconomic model were based on analysis of contacts reported on a citizen survey and used an individual rather than an areal unit of analysis.

These differences are especially important in the light of Verba and Nie's (1972) distinction between "particularized" and "general referent" contacts. As Kenneth Mladenka (1978: 13) aptly notes, bureaucracies are unlikely to record "contacts which express a general policy preference" whereas "particularized requests," which are referred through normal bureaucratic processing channels, are likely to be recorded. Consequently, the study of agency-recorded contacts is likely to be primarily a study of particularized contacting, and the study of survey-reported contacts is likely to include both general referent and particularized contacts. If Verba and Nie (1972) are correct in their assertion that these two types of contacting are substantially different forms of behavior, subject to different explanatory models, the choice of data-collection strategy can critically affect the findings about contacting.

Apart from the effect that data-collection strategy has on the types of contacts that are analyzed, methodological differences might also lead to conflicting findings because of differences in the unit of analysis. Since bureaucracies do not usually record demographic characteristics of the individual contactor (or measure the citizen's political attitudes), studies relying on archival data aggregate contacts to an areal unit such as the census tract and relate contacting propensity (in the sense of a count of contacts from a given area) to variation in such census tract characteristics as average value of housing, age of housing, or distance from the city center—all proxy measures of the social "well-being" or social status of the area. Survey-based studies, on the other hand, typically focus heavily on individual characteristics, such as income, educational attainment, race, political interest, and the like. Analysis proceeds by correlating individual propensity to contact (whether the individual has made a contact in the recent past) with these individual attributes.

In sum, different data-collection methods imply different units of analysis; and different units of analysis require different definitions of contacting propensity and focus attention on somewhat different independent variables. Apart from these differences, it is possible, as Vedlitz and Veblen (1980: 60) suggest in their analysis of the need-awareness model, that a model that works at the aggregate level may not be appropriately adapted to individual behavior.

Several reactions to these alternative models and the conflicting findings they have generated are possible. One is strategic retreat from the effort to disentangle the conflict. Another is a renewed search for evidence that will soundly disconfirm one or the other of the two models. The analysis of contacting in Kansas City presented here is guided by a third alternative—the assumption that some synthesis of the socioeconomic model and the need-awareness model is possible and desirable. Although each of these models represents elegant simplicity, neither provides a very comprehensive explanation, nor has either model alone successfully accounted for patterns of contacting in a variety of settings.

Despite the obvious obstacles, some progress toward synthesis already exists. John Thomas, for example, suggests that "citizen-initiated contacts with government agencies will be a function primarily of perceived needs, an individual's instrumental concerns, and secondarily of the socioeconomic model, presumably the general political attitudes and information that also affect traditional forms of political participation" (1982: 518). In his analysis of contacting in Cincinnati, Thomas (1982) found evidence for this interpretation, which blends elements of the need-awareness model with the socioeconomic model.

Much more must be done to sort out the interconnections between the two models and to explore potentially important factors overlooked by both models. Figure 1-3 illustrates the conceptual framework that will be pursued here. It should not be viewed as a causal model, to be tested in toto. Rather, it serves as a map of the analytical terrain that will be pursued.

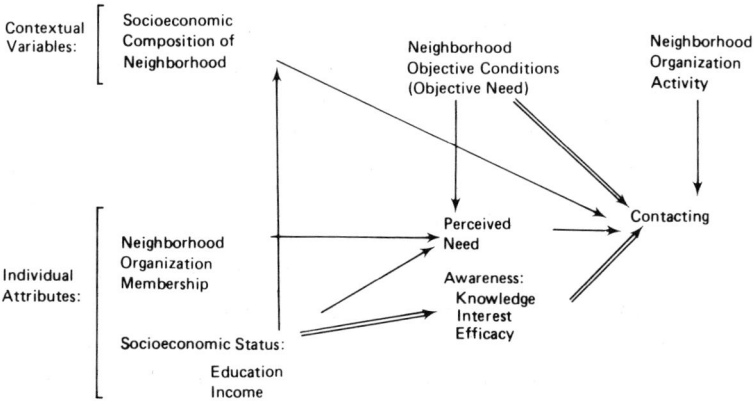

FIGURE 1-3. *A Synthetic Model of Contacting Propensity*

Chapter 2, for example, initiates the search for a synthesis by applying both the socioeconomic model and the need-awareness model to individual contacting behavior. The limitations of both models are explored, and the reasons for the failure of the socioeconomic model are outlined. At least some of these have relevance for the need-awareness model also, as Figure 1-3 suggests. The double-lined arrows in the figure highlight the relationships that are the focus of the socioeconomic and need-awareness models. From this, at least one aspect of a synthesis is evident: both models posit that a set of political attitudes or orientations, such as knowledge about government, political interest, and efficacy, are critical explanatory factors. In the socioeconomic model, these serve as mediating factors between socioeconomic status and political mobilization; these same attitudes and orientations constitute the awareness component of the need-awareness model. The relative weakness of these attitudes as predictors of contacting propensity, and the relative strength of perceived need, are the major findings of Chapter 2.

Jones and colleagues' (1977) original formulation of the need-awareness model is based on objective needs, but others (Thomas, 1982) have argued that perceived need is a more appropriate concept for explaining political activation. The link between objective need and perceived need has not been adequately explored. As Figure 1-3 illustrates, perceived need may be largely a function of objective conditions; but it is also possible that other factors impinge upon citizens' expectations and therefore upon perceived need. Socioeconomic status and membership in neighborhood organizations, for example, may condition expectations and therefore have an impact on perceived need. These possibilities are examined in Chapter 3.

Apart from objective conditions in the neighborhood, there are other potentially important contextual variables that have not heretofore been incorporated in either the socioeconomic or need-awareness models. Like other forms of political participation, contacting may be contingent on the social context of the neighborhood as well as individual attributes. The power of the socioeconomic model, for example, cannot be clearly assessed without some attention to the socioeconomic composition of the neighborhood in which the individual resides. In addition, neighborhood organizations are frequently assumed to play a role in mobilizing residents for demand-making (Yates, 1977; O'Brien, 1975). Yet the impact of neighborhood organizations on citizen-initiated contacting has not been documented, even though the need-awareness model provides an excellent framework for isolating "exceptional" neighborhoods, where unexpected levels of contacting might be traceable to activity by neighborhood organizations. Indeed, in an exceptional effort to test for the effect of neighborhood organizations on demand-making, Jones (1981: 696) found no evidence in Chicago that community organizations have a stimulative effect on demand-making.

Chapter 3 shifts to a contextual form of analysis to explore the various issues outlined above. The socioeconomic model is reexamined within the context of neighborhood socioeconomic composition, the roots of perceived need are explored, and the role of neighborhood organizations is assessed through comparative case analysis.

Chapter 4 explores the possibility that centralized complaint-handling units, such as the one in Kansas City, may make a difference in the citizen-initiated contacting process. Variations in channels of access to city government are examined, and differences in citizen evaluations of the handling of their request or complaint highlight the possiblity that centralized complaint units can enhance the responsiveness of local government.

The final two chapters explore various aspects of the significance of citizen-initiated contacting in urban politics. Contacting represents one form of demand-making, or what Albert Hirschman (1970) calls the "voice option." Voice, however, is not the only possible response to problems in the community. Hirschman (1970) argues that "exit, voice, and loyalty" form a triumvirate of possible responses for discontented citizens and that these options are interrelated. The extent to which the exit option is used, for example, may be contingent on the availability and viability of the voice option. From this perspective, patterns of citizen-initiated contacting and evaluations of government responsiveness to them are part of the politics of the limited city (Peterson, 1981), which cannot control mobility but must compete to hold the allegiance of higher-than-average taxpaying citizens. Chapter 5 elaborates on these themes.

Finally, Chapter 6 sets the findings about demand-making in the urban context against the larger debate about the demand-oriented character of current American politics. An ethic of self-reliance is said to constrain the American public from politicizing many personal problems (Sniderman and Brody, 1977). Other analysts argue that American politics currently is based on expectations that virtually all forms of personal risk should be "socialized" (Aharoni, 1981) and that there is an overload of demands for government intervention to solve a variety of personal problems. Chapter 6 provides an argument that the rhetoric of the city reform movement and the institutional structures that evolved from it (including centralized complaint units) lend themselves to a special public ethic operating in urban politics—an ethic more in line with the high-demand interpretations of American politics than with analyses of the power of a self-reliance ethic.

Before proceeding to the analysis, however, an explanation of the setting for the research and the choice of study neighborhoods is in order. The following section attends to this and some preliminary data-collection issues.

Research Setting: City, Complaint Bureau, and Study Neighborhoods

Kansas City, Missouri—the site for this study—is a medium-sized city (1980 population of about 480,000). It is part of a ten-county Consolidated Metropolitan Statistical Area that includes Kansas City, Kansas, and several counties on both sides of the Kansas-Missouri border. Like many research sites, it was chosen not because it is inherently representative of American cities but because it was accessible and has a centralized complaint-handling unit.

The Action Center

Kansas City's centralized complaint-handling unit, called the Action Center, was established in 1974, partly in response to recommendations by a research institute that had been commissioned to study city hall communications. Two council members, other city staff members, and a consultant from the research institute visited complaint- and request-handling units already instituted in St. Petersburg, Florida, and Dallas, Texas, and modeled Kansas City's unit on them.

The Action Center is housed in the office of the city manager. According to the city's "Guide to Action Center Operations," its goals are to serve as an information resource for citizens who are not familiar with city regulations, services, or organization; serve as a central point of contact for citizens to request city services or to provide important input to city management; and provide an easily accessible, sincerely interested, and unbiased point of contact at the managerial level for citizens who feel that the city is not meeting their needs.

The Action Center deals with requests both for information and service and with complaints. Roughly two-thirds of the approximately forty-five thousand contacts that the Action Center receives each year are requests for information. These are handled directly by the Action Center staff—information is provided, and very little documentation of the contact is made.

The requests or complaints regarding service provide most of the Action Center's activity. About fifteen thousand of these are received each year. When the Action Center receives a contact concerning a service delivery problem, a service request form describing the problem and location is completed and sent to the appropriate city department. In addition, the Action Center opens a case file on the service request, through which action on the problem is tracked. In consultation with city departments, the Action Center has established a set of standardized time periods for the resolution of various service delivery problems. Consequently, when the service request is referred to the appropriate department, an expected time of completion, or "suspense date," is also assigned to the case. Departments are expected either to complete action and report back to the Action Center by that date or to request an extension, stipulating the reasons an extension is needed. On the basis of the suspense date, the Action Center notifies the citizen of what action is to be taken and the due date.

When the department reports back to the Action Center that its activity concerning the case is completed (either the service has been delivered and the problem resolved or no action has been taken because of jurisdictional issues or no problem was found), the Action Center codes the resolution accordingly and closes the case. The center also sends the citizen a postcard, asking for an evaluation of the handling of the problem. All cases on which postcards are returned with unfavorable ratings are followed up by one staff specialist, who visits the site of the problem and attempts to document whether in fact a resolvable problem has been left unattended. Finally, data from the Action Center are used in regular merit evaluations of city department heads, and summary information on case load, case type, and resolution, broken down by councilmanic district, is provided to city council members.

In short, Kansas City's Action Center exemplifies the centralized complaint-handling institutions that have emerged in many cities. Its functions are virtually identical to those summarized by Gellhorn: "Many cities have also established a central office in which complaints can be lodged. This facilitates the citizen's communications with the city; it also makes possible a systematic 'follow up' that assures suitable action on the complaint and, in due course, a report to the complainant; and, finally, the central office's tabulations reveal to the city's chief administrator (its manager, mayor or other executive) patterns of complaint that suggest where a bit of supervisory polish should be applied" (1966: 160).

The Action Center has not totally replaced other channels for the citizen to contact city hall. Rather, it is a new institutional arrangement, overlaid upon an existing pattern of contacts with city council members, the mayor's office, department heads, and the like. The significance of such a complaint unit depends on the extent to which it can change the aggregate pattern of citizen demand-making by offering an alternative for groups unlikely to use other channels and the extent to which citizens' perceptions of government responsiveness are enhanced when problems are handled by such a unit. These potential impacts are explored in Chapter 4.

Kansas City as a Research Site

In some ways, Kansas City may be unrepresentative of the majority of American cities. It was historically the site of one of the handful of truly noteworthy political machines—the Pendergast machine, which dominated its city politics from the 1890s to 1939. Currently, the city has the council-manager form of government, and in this respect, too, it is unusual—it is one of the relatively few American cities of its size to have this form of government.

Apart from its centralized complaint-handling unit, however, Kansas City provides an interesting laboratory for the study of patterns of citizens' contacts with government officials. It has a relatively rich neighborhood tradition, reflected in the mix of neighborhood types described below and in the variety of neighborhood organizations. Exploring the role of these organizations in the demand-making process is an important part of this analysis.

In addition, the everyday strains of service delivery in the face of budget constraints have taken on an added urgency because Kansas City faces the problems of an aging infrastructure. The collapse of a portion of one bridge and the closing of several others in recent years, coming on the heels of a major catastrophe when a skywalk collapsed in a local hotel and an earlier problem when the roof of Kemper Arena blew off, led one local newspaper columnist to dub Kansas City "the amazing crumbling city." The designation may be unfair but it suggests that, like many older cities, Kansas City is currently in a period of heightened consciousness regarding its basic infrastructure.

Finally, the sweep of change that the reform movement brought to American cities is visibly written on the institutional face of Kansas City, and the city's experiences exemplify many of the ongoing challenges faced by these reform government institutions. Many Kansas Citians are proud that their community rid itself of the Pendergast machine, replacing it with a professional city government administered by a city manager. Representational issues have been resolved through a hybrid arrangement in which six of the city's twelve council members are elected at-large and the other six are elected from districts.

But many of the thorny problems of city government remain. During the period of this study, a major controversy erupted when a local newspaper uncovered evidence of falsification of records and other employee misconduct in the Codes Administration Division of the city's Department of Public Works. Earlier the same year, money was reported missing from the City Water Department.

These high-visibility, management-oriented controversies are the exception rather than the rule in Kansas City. More frequently, local politics revolves around development issues. Like many other cities, Kansas City is struggling to revitalize its downtown and to bring in new commerce, industry, and jobs. Reports of possible new downtown development projects and efforts to provide financing for them are regular fare for that portion of the public that is attentive to city government issues.

Perhaps the most routine aspect of city politics, however, is the politics of service delivery. Although not always newsworthy, allocation and quality of what Paul Peterson (1981) calls the basic "housekeeping" services are ongoing issues in Kansas City politics. In some areas of the city, peculiarities of development exacerbate these issues. Kansas City annexed outward in the 1960s, both northward and southward, and questions about the quality of services in these areas readily surface, especially at election time.

Complaints from citizens of the "northland" and the "southland" are only one aspect of the politics of service delivery in Kansas City. The city is also subject to pressure from residents of core city neighborhoods who believe their neighborhoods have been prematurely written off by the city, labor showdowns with the firefighters' union, broad-based citizen disaffection when heavy storms tax the city's snow removal capacity, and many other conflicts and issues revolving around the delivery of basic urban services.

If Kansas City is therefore an appealing site for the study of citizens' complaints and service requests, it is also a challenge. Because a key purpose of this research is to provide a synthesis of the two major explanatory models of citizen-initiated contacts, a research design was needed that employed multimethod datacollection strategies and had the capacity for meaningful analysis with both individual and aggregate spatial units of analysis. The multimethod features of the design will be described shortly. Here it is important to consider the definition and selection of the spatial units of analysis.

THE KANSAS CITY STUDY NEIGHBORHOODS

Neighborhoods are significant units of analysis for the study of urban service demands and responses. As Yates (1977) notes, urban services are locality-specific. Different neighborhoods may have different needs for service, urban administrators make decisions about deployment of service on a neighborhood basis, and citizens tend to generate demands for service in accordance with their experiences. In addition, organizations representing neighborhood areas may play an important role in generating demands for service.

In their Detroit study, Jones and colleagues (1977) used the census tract as a spatial unit of analysis. Census tracts, however, do not necessarily correspond with neighborhoods. The ease of obtaining demographic data for census tracts is traded off against the loss of socially meaningful spatial units.

How, then, does one define neighborhoods for the purpose of studying patterns of citizen-initiated contacting? There is no consensus in the social sciences about the appropriate operational definition of neighborhood, partly because conceptualizations of the neighborhood range from sociological ones (in which shared experiences and social networks are important) to psychological ones (in which subjective attachment is the important criterion) to physical or administrative ones (which emphasize distinctive land-use areas or the geographic boundaries of local service districts or facilities) (Keller, 1968).

Relying on locally recognized, named subareas of the city has its own pitfalls, as shown by a Kansas City newspaper columnist's description of the confusions involved:

> In Kansas City, its awfully difficult to know where you're coming from. History and loose talk have turned the city's neighborhood and district names into a hopelessly confusing hodgepodge. When Kansas City expanded significantly into the area north of the river, the term "Kansas City, North" was adopted to distinguish it from other cities there. . . . The Northland became a generic term for north of the river, but nobody has been able to determine how far north. . . . The North End . . . was a term referring to the area north of the present Downtown loop but south of the river. In time, however, the "North End" came to be associated with corrupt politics and gangsters. So the term was phased out in favor of the North Side. [Arthur S. Brisbane, "What Is in a Name? Confusion," *Kansas City Times*, June 25, 1982, p. B1]

As these comments indicate, there is considerable disagreement about the precise boundaries of various "neighborhoods" and considerable variation in the place names used to refer to subareas of the city. But this confusion highlights the importance of spatial differentiation in Kansas City. As in most American cities, Kansas City has a sociopolitical geography that must be considered by the urban analyst because it is significant to the people who live there.

This significance is apparent in Richard Coleman and Bernice Neugarten's (1971) study of social status in Kansas City, based on their research done there in the mid-1950s. They note that "whenever Kansas City people talked about stratification systems more complex than those based on wealth, collar-color lines, or ethnic grouping, they almost invariably turned to residential geography. Most persons identified at least five levels of neighborhoods, and many identified six or seven. Residential address was considered the quickest index to a family's social status" (1971: 30). Thus neighborhoods are socially and politically meaningful units of analysis, but to formulate an operational definition of what constitutes a neighborhood is always a challenge. Apart from the problems noted above, Kansas City is subdivided in one manner for purposes of political representation, in another for the service delivery organization such as trash collection zones and police districts, and still another is needed to represent active neighborhood organization boundaries. The researcher interested in obtaining demographic data cannot totally ignore census tracts, which provide yet another mapping of the city, and the Action Center codes its data by Zip Code area.

The definition of study neighborhoods for this analysis is conditioned by this crazy-quilt pattern of relevant subarea mappings but is keyed primarily to neighborhood organization boundaries on the assumption that they represent the best local, socially meaningful, residential subareas. In effect, a City Development Department map of the boundaries of various community organizations was superimposed on the other relevant mappings. Study neighborhoods were then pieced together in such a way that each (1) is maximally faithful to neighborhood organization boundaries, (2) results in a total study neighborhood population of no more than ten thousand, (3) incorporates census tracts or portions thereof with similar housing values and minority-white ratios, and (4) falls within a single Zip Code area. Some might argue that a subarea with a population of ten thousand is too large to constitute a neighborhood. In fact, all but five of the study neighborhoods are considerably smaller—less than six thousand population—and four of the other five are between six and seven thousand population. Only one (Easterling) is at the top end of the range. Even neighborhoods of five or six thousand population would perhaps seem objectionably large to those who conceptualize the neighborhood as having close, neighboring networks. Here, however, the overriding consideration in defining neighborhoods is the neighborhood organization and its geographical boundaries. Typically, neighborhood organizations encompass somewhat larger areas than those that would be entailed by other definitions.

Study neighborhoods were not chosen randomly. Rather, a selection matrix, incorporating percent black and average housing value, was used to isolate a set of twenty-four neighborhoods meeting all of the above criteria and proportionately representing the city's census tracts on these two criteria as well. In addition, selections were made to include several study neighborhoods from each councilmanic district, a constraint that is important because service delivery issues differ in the core districts and the further out areas of the "northland" and "southland."

As Figure 1-4 indicates, a plurality of Kansas City census tracts are less than 10 percent black and have average housing values in a range suggesting lower-middle to upper-middle income occupants ($25,000 to $65,000); correspondingly, the largest number of neighborhoods (42 percent) are in this category. About one-fifth of Kansas City census tracts have majority black populations and average housing values under $25,000; so five of the twenty-four study neighborhoods (21 percent) are of this type. Relatively few census tracts are either racially mixed with low housing values, racially mixed with moderate housing values, predominantly white with low housing values, or predominantly white with high housing values. Correspondingly, only two to three neighborhoods of each type are represented in the set of study neighborhoods. Since no census tracts are either racially mixed with high housing values or predominantly black with high housing values, and a negligible proportion are predominantly black with moderate housing values, no study neighborhoods of any of these types are represented. The neighborhood names used are pseudonyms to ensure the anonymity that was promised to the neighborhood organization leaders interviewed for this study; actual neighborhood names in most cases would reveal the neigh-

FIGURE 1-4. *Selection Matrix for the Study Neighborhoods*

Average Value of Housing (1980)	Percent Black Population (1980)		
	0–10	11–50	51 or more
Less than $25,000	10 percent of census tracts 8 percent of study neighborhoods Southton* Lester	10 percent of census tracts 12.5 percent of study neighborhoods Valleyglen Valleydale Dupree	22 percent of census tracts 21 percent of study neighborhoods Belton Bluewood Ivy Hill Easterling Westview
$25,000–$65,000	40 percent of census tracts 42 percent of study neighborhoods Lemon Hill West Park Littleton Greenbriar Wentworth Friar Road Jackson Rambeau Broadview Weston	7 percent of census tracts 8 percent of study neighborhoods Risley Highland	1 percent of census tracts no study neighborhoods
$65,000 or more	10 percent of census tracts 8 percent of study neighborhoods Clover Downs Robard	0 percent of census tracts no study neighborhoods	0 percent of census tracts no study neighborhoods

*Pseudonyms are used rather than actual neighborhood names.

borhood organizations as well and therefore the identity of respondents. In sum, the definition and selection of study neighborhoods is intended to provide a diverse set, yet one that is proportionately representative of the racial composition and housing values shown in the distribution of Kansas City census tracts. The set of study neighborhoods is mapped in Figure 1-5, which shows their geographic spread across the councilmanic districts. Although there are at least two study neighborhoods in each of the six councilmanic districts, the study neighborhoods are not evenly distributed across or within the districts. This distribution reflects the primacy of proportional representation on the racial composition and housing value criteria and the deliberate effort to choose areas that, in addition, fit established neighborhood organization boundaries with minimal crossing of census tract and Zip Code area boundaries.

The definition of socially meaningful spatial units of analysis is one of the ways in which the research is designed to permit analysis of alternative explanations derived from both individual-level and spatial analysis. In addition, a multimethod approach incorporating both survey data and archival data from the city's Action Center is a crucial feature. Random sample citizen surveys were conducted in each of the twenty-four study neighborhoods (see Appendix A for a description of the survey design and administration), and information from the Action Center's case files was collected and geo-coded to these study neighborhoods. These data sources are supplemented by in-depth interviews of leaders of neighborhood organizations in each of the areas, census data "matched up" to the study neighborhoods, ratings by trained observers of a variety of neighborhood conditions, and various forms of city archival data other than the Action Center's.

These varied data sets, coupled with the identification of a set of study neighborhoods, allow for analysis of demand-making based on both individual behavior and neighborhood propen-

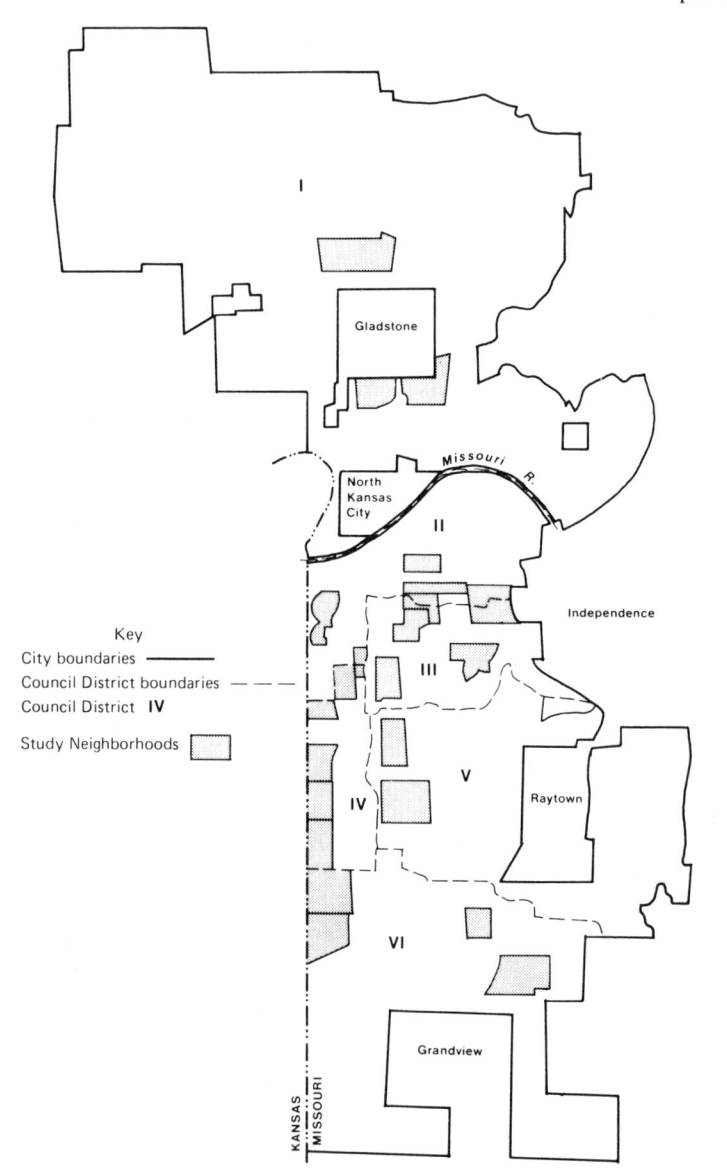

FIGURE 1-5. *Kansas City Study Neighborhoods*

sities. The design also permits examination of the contacting phenomenon as captured in citizen self-reports and in the records of a centralized complaint bureau.

2

Patterns of Contacting: The Socioeconomic and the Need-Awareness Models

☑ ☐ ☐
☑ ☐ ☐

An obvious starting point for analysis of patterns of citizen-initiated contacting is the question, Who makes such contacts? This question takes us directly to a test of the socioeconomic model, which specifies that upper-status citizens—the better educated, those with higher incomes, and perhaps white residents—should be more prone to making such contacts than lower-status citizens. Tables 2-1 and 2-2 show that, although there is some evidence of the patterns that the model would predict, the explanatory power of this model is limited. Although contacting does increase somewhat among persons of higher income and education, the associations between each of these variables and contacting are very low. There are virtually no differences across racial groups in the propensity to contact local government officials.

It is possible, however, that this is not a fair test of the socioeconomic model. Verba and Nie (1972), for example, have argued that contacts are not all alike. They come in two varieties: particularized contacts, which involve matters of primary concern to the individual contactors or their families (such as getting one's trash collected, a complaint about how the police responded to one's call for assistance, or a request that dead tree limbs be removed from one's property) and "general referent" contacts, which involve matters of wider concern to the community (such as a demand for increased police patrols in residential areas after dark or a demand that residential streets have repaving priority over commercial streets). Verba and Nie (1972) found that par-

TABLE 2-1. *Socioeconomic Characteristics of Persons Who Had Contacted a City Official in the Last Year*

By Income (in 000's of $)	Percent (N)	By Education	Percent (N)
Under 10	26 (575)	Less than 12 years	26 (443)
10–20	29 (453)	12 years	24 (689)
20–30	32 (355)	13–16 years	31 (803)
30–40	29 (182)	Over 16 years	39 (193)
40–50	40 (87)		
Over 50	39 (64)		

Gamma = .11 Gamma = .14
Kendall's Tau_b = .07 Kendall's Tau_b = .07
Pearson's r = .07 Sig. < .01 Pearson's r = .08 Sig. < .01

TABLE 2-2. *Race of Persons Who Had Contacted a City Official in the Last Year*

Race	Percent	(N)
Whites	28	(1,608)
Blacks	28	(391)
Other	32	(115)

Chi^2 = .85 Sig. = .65

ticularized contacting is peculiarly not amenable to explanation via the socioeconomic model. General referent contacting, on the other hand, is part of a communal participation dimension (along with activities such as working with neighbors on local problems), and communal participation is not an exception to the standard socioeconomic model. Perhaps, then, the weak association between overall contacting and socioeconomic status (SES) could be resolved into two distinctive patterns: a negligible SES-particularized contacting relationship and a positive SES-general referent contacting relationship.

To distinguish particularized from general referent contactors, the citizen survey asked each respondent who said he or she had contacted a government official whether the contact was about something concerning the individual or the household or something of concern to the community generally. Those giving the former response are categorized as particularized contactors; those giving the latter are categorized as general referent contactors. Overall, 28 percent of the respondents said that they had made a contact with a government official in the past year. The bulk of these (69 percent), however, were general referent contacts; only 31 percent of those who had made a contact said it was a matter of concern primarily to themselves or their family (i.e., particularized). This means that particularized contacting is a relatively rarely self-reported behavior for the sample as a whole—only 8.5% of all respondents said they had made such a contact. General referent contacting was a more commonly reported behavior —18.7 percent of all respondents said they had made such a contact.

One could speculate, of course, that this distribution of types of contacts is a function of a social desirability response when citizens are asked to characterize their own motivations for approaching city hall. Presumably, most citizens would prefer to represent themselves as acting in the public interest, rather than for their own narrow interests. Using a very different method to distinguish particularized from general referent contacts (content analysis of the matter about which the respondent contacted an official), however, Verba and Nie (1972) found a virtually identical breakdown of general referent and particularized contacts.

It is at least as likely, then, that if there is distortion in these self-reports, it is not so much in definition of the character of reported contacts with city hall as in gaps in recalling particularized contacts. Making a demand involving a large policy issue is surely more memorable than the more routine help-seeking or service-requesting that constitutes particularized contacting. As further evidence, various researchers report different levels of survey-reported contacting, depending upon the method used to solicit responses. In this study and those by Verba and Nie (1972) and Sharp (1982), the proportion of respondents who said they had made a contact ranged from one-fifth to one-third. In his Cincinnati study, however, Thomas (1982) found a majority of respondents (54.7 percent) reporting a contact with city government. The difference, as Thomas (1982: 508) notes, is that he broke down contacts into a variety of service areas (police, fire, traffic, parks, and the like), and the questions about contacts followed a series of questions about aspects of those services. Such an arrangement may be expected to stimulate recall about routine, particularized contacts that a more general survey item would miss.

Apart from the issue of recall, the use of self-reports of the referent for the contact as a means of distinguishing particularized from general referent contactors might be challenged because Verba and Nie's (1972) initial operationalization of the concept entailed content coding based on the generality of the problem. There are two reasons for the alternative approach used here— one practical and one theoretical.

The practical matter is that it would be difficult in many cases to distinguish narrow from general problems in the fashion Verba and Nie (1972) suggest. When respondents indicate that they called about a flooding problem or poor garbage collection, for example, the problems, and hence the contacts, could be narrow matters, having to do with the individual's own basement flooding or garbage collection being handled poorly; they could just as easily involve widespread flooding problems in the neighborhood or perceptions that unsightly, spilled garbage is marring the image of many of the city's residential neighborhoods. Perhaps Verba and Nie's (1972) survey interviewers were able to probe more fully to clarify the difference in such cases; such information is not, however, consistently available here.

There is a theoretical reason, as well, for focusing on the citizen's notion of the referent for the contact (self or community) rather than an objective coding of the generality of the contact problem. Citizens may or may not be knowledgeable about the scope of the problem as the researcher sees it or motivated to contact on this basis. Consider, for example, two individuals who call to complain about the quality of garbage collection. A researcher would be likely to classify this as a low-generality problem and hence a particularized contact. One of the citizens may, indeed, fit this characterization, having called the city only with the intent of getting his or her own garbage collected properly in the future. The other, however, may view his or her own problem as just one example of poor-quality garbage collection service throughout the city. The problem, in other words, is for the contactor a broader one, reflecting quality-control problems in the city bureaucracy that threaten the quality of life in many neighborhoods. This contactor may hope to have an impact on the quality of garbage collection generally.

Mundane as this example may be, it illustrates the importance of the contactor's perceptions and intentions in the demand-making process. Making a demand concerning an ostensibly broad-scope problem surely does not qualify one as a civic-minded, communal participant if one's intentions have to do only with the personal impacts of that problem; similarly, making a demand concerning a problem that might appear to be narrow in scope surely does not qualify one as a parochial, particularistic contactor if one actually had in mind some broader ramifications of the problem. In this light, using survey reports of the referent that the citizen had in mind is perhaps more consistent with Verba and Nie's (1972) conceptualization of particularistic versus general referent contacting than their own efforts to operationalize this through objective coding of the scope of the problem.

The distinction between particularized and general referent contacting is significant only insofar as the two are distinctive forms of political assertion. Verba and Nie (1972: 66) were the first to argue this question, claiming that contacting is the only form of assertion in which the individual can "'set the agenda' for his political act." Whether the contact is used to obtain a narrow benefit for the individual or to make a demand that more broadly affects the community is a critical distinction for Verba and Nie.

The socioeconomic model would be expected to work for general referent contacting because the scope of the outcome of this mode approximates that of other modes of participation. Particularized contacting, on the other hand, should not be a function of the socioeconomic variables that predict other, more civic-oriented modes of political participation. Table 2-3, however, forces us to reject this line of argument. Socioeconomic variables are no better predictors of general referent contacting than of particularized contacting. So the overall weakness of the socioeconomic model in accounting for contacting is not attributable to the lumping together of both types of contacts. A deeper explanation for the weakness of the socioeconomic model must be found.

TABLE 2-3. *Relationships Between Socioeconomic Variables and Various Forms of Contacting Behavior*

Type of Contacting	Education Gamma	r	Income Gamma	r
Particularized contacting	.09	.04*	.10	.05*
General referent contacting	.11	.07†	.09	.05*
Any contacting	.12	.09†	.11	.08†

*Significant at less than .05 level.
†Significant at less than .01 level.

Why Does the Socioeconomic Model Falter?

Insofar as traditional measures of socioeconomic status such as education and income are relatively weak predictors of contacting, we must conclude that the socioeconomic model is not particularly suitable to account for this form of demand-making. But it is worth considering why the socioeconomic model falters. The model does not simply specify that higher-status individuals are more prone to a variety of political behaviors. It also specifies that this occurs because higher-status individuals are more likely to develop the political attitudes and competencies that are prerequisites for participation. These intervening attitudes and skills account for the link between SES and political involvement in the standard socioeconomic model.

This elaboration suggests two possible reasons for the weakness of the socioeconomic model in the case of contacting behavior: (1) the political attitudes and skills that are important prerequisites for other forms of participation are not as relevant for contacting; (2) these political attitudes and skills are important predictors of contacting, but they are not a function of socioeconomic status, at least in the urban setting of the 1980s. The former explanation suggests that contacting is a unique form of behavior, distinct from other modes of political assertion. Verba and Nie (1972), for example, draw this conclusion from their analysis. The latter explanation suggests that established views about the development and distribution of political attitudes and skills may not be as applicable in the current urban scene.

To explore these possibilities, three political attitudes or skills that the socioeconomic model incorporates as key intervening factors between SES and participation will be examined: efficacy, interest in government, and knowledge of government. Measures of each of these variables were designed for appropriateness of application to analysis of an *urban* political phenomenon.

For example, a political efficacy scale developed by Mitchell Seligson (1980) is used rather than more commonly accepted efficacy scales because the latter are geared toward the individual's sense of potential impact on politics more generally.[1] The Seligson scale first required the respondents to identify an important problem in the community. Then the respondents were asked how the problem came about, who could help to solve the problem, and whether or not they themselves could help to solve the problem. Efficacious responses included the capacity to define a problem, to give an explanation of the problem, to identify a source of solution, and an affirmative response on whether or not they could help solve the problem. Overall,

48 percent of Kansas City respondents were classified as low on efficacy—that is, not able to specify an important community problem; about one-fifth (19 percent) of the respondents scored high on this efficacy scale by providing efficacious responses to all four items; the remaining third of the respondents were categorized as moderate on this efficacy scale.

Interest in government was assessed by a single survey item, which asked, "How interested would you say you are in the operations of city government?" Response categories ranged from "very interested" to "somewhat interested" to "not at all interested." Overall, 30 percent of the respondents said they were "very interested" in city government, 61 percent were "somewhat" interested, and 9 percent were "not at all" interested.

Finally, knowledge of government was assessed through a series of items asking respondents to name the mayor, the city manager, a council member for their district, any other city council member, and whether they knew about the city's central complaints unit, the Action Center.[2] The knowledge of government scale used here is a count of the number of correct responses to these five items. Overall, 14 percent of the respondents knew none of these and 28 percent knew only one; 25 percent could name two, 16 percent knew three, 11 percent knew four, and only 6 percent knew all five.

Before proceeding to analysis of how these political attitudes and competencies relate to SES variables on the one hand and contacting on the other, it is important to note that specification of these possible intervening variables carries us a step toward synthesis of the socioeconomic model with the need-awareness model. In their discussion of the awareness dimension, for example, Jones and colleagues note that "a number of studies have found that persons of high status and education tend to have more knowledge and greater sophistication about government and politics than do their lower-status counterparts" (1977: 51). The studies referred to are the building blocks of the socioeconomic model, and the notions of civic competence, political sophistication, and attentiveness to politics with which they deal are encapsulated by Jones and colleagues in the "awareness" concept; they are also reflected in the set of intervening variables to be analyzed here. Both the socioeconomic model and the awareness component of Jones's need-awareness model hinge upon strong associations between SES variables and these political attitudes and competencies.

Taken together, Tables 2-4 and 2-5 suggest why the socioeconomic model breaks down in the case of contacting. Table 2-4 shows that only one of these variables—efficacy—is a strong predictor of contacting behavior; Table 2-5 shows, however, that SES variables are weakly associated with political efficacy. Political interest is modestly associated with contacting, but the SES-interest relationship is weak. Knowledge of city government officials comes closest to what the socioeconomic model suggests, for there are modest relationships between SES variables and knowledge on the one hand, and between knowledge and contacting on the other. Neither linkage, however, is particularly strong.

In sum, these data suggest that there is some truth to both of the possible reasons specified earlier for the weakness of the socioeconomic model. Depending upon which form of political awareness is at issue, either the link to SES variables is negligible or the link to contacting propensity is weaker than might be expected. Of the three measures of political awareness, however, knowledge of government officials comes closest to performing as the socioeconomic model would predict.

Several additional comments on Tables 2-4 and 2-5 are in order. It should perhaps not be surprising that level of political efficacy turns out to be a stronger predictor of contacting behavior than interest in local government or knowledge of government officials. Contacting is usually conceptualized as an instrumental form of behavior (Thomas, 1982), and it is surely less tinged with overtones of civic duty than are such forms of participation as voting. From this perspective, having an interest in city government affairs need not be a prerequisite or even a motivator for

TABLE 2-4. *Contacting and Political Awareness*

A. Percent and (N) Who Contacted	by	Level of Political Efficacy		
		Low	Moderate	High
		18	31	48
		(1,027)	(707)	(414)
			Gamma = .43	
			Kendall's Tau$_b$ = .23	
			Pearson's r = .25	
B. Percent and (N) Who Contacted	by	Interest in City Government		
		Not at All	Somewhat	Very
		18	27	35
		(189)	(1,278)	(632)
			Gamma = .24	
			Kendall's Tau$_b$ = .11	
			Pearson's r = .12	
C. Percent and (N) Who Contacted	by	Knowledge (Number of Government Entities Known)		
		0–1	2–3	4–5
		24	27	43
		(897)	(876)	(375)
			Gamma = .23	
			Kendall's Tau$_b$ = .12	
			Pearson's r = .13	

TABLE 2-5. *Socioeconomic Status and Political Awareness*

Variable Pairing	Gamma	Pearson's r	(N)
Efficacy and education	.15	.12	(2,118)
Interest and education	.11	.08	(2,078)
Knowledge and education	.32	.27	(2,118)
Efficacy and income	.01	.03	(1,724)
Interest and income	.02	.02	(1,699)
Knowledge and income	.29	.23	(1,724)

contacting city officials with complaints or requests about service delivery. Knowledge of who government officials are can, in one sense, be seen as an indicator of the ease with which one could reach city hall with a complaint or request. Yet, by the same token, this need not be a particularly important stepping stone for contacting behavior. The citizen may have other avenues for access to city hall than the key officials asked about here, such as city department personnel or a simple call to city hall with the expectation of referral to the appropriate office. After all, the rhetoric of the reform movement in city government suggests that you do not need to know anyone personally in city government to get a response. Clout is out and administration through neutral competence is in.

One's sense of political efficacy, however, has been found to be a key to other forms of participation (Neal and Seeman, 1964; Gamson, 1968; Campbell, Gurin, and Miller, 1954 and 1960). The relative power of this variable in predicting contacting behavior should not be surprising because, as Verba and Nie (1972: 52) aptly note, contacting, perhaps even more than other modes of participation, requires personal initiative. The occasion for assertion is not presented to the citizen, as it is in voting for example, but must be defined by the citizen. A sense of political competence, which is what the efficacy concept entails, is a likely prerequisite for such a relatively difficult act of political assertion.

On the SES–political attitudes side of the model (Table 2-5), negligible relationships between SES variables and both interest in city government and sense of political efficacy are somewhat surprising. These measures, however, were designed to tap interest in city government and political efficacy within a local context. More traditionally used measures of political efficacy focus on a more general political context, and responses are likely to be in reference to the federal government or to politics more generally. That interest in city government is not a function of income or education and that level of political efficacy is surprisingly unhinged from SES variables may signal that basic orientations toward political life in the local context differ from political

Patterns of Contacting   43

orientations in a larger, national context. It is surely not farfetched to imagine that many citizens who do not believe they can understand, let alone have an impact on, national political affairs would feel far from helpless or inept in the local setting (Balch, 1974).

In short, the weakness of the socioeconomic model in the case of contacting is in large part attributable to the absence of a systematic connection between SES and political attitudes with respect to the urban community. We need not conclude, then, as have Verba and Nie (1972), that contacting is simply a maverick form of political assertion. The weakness of the socioeconomic model points at least as strongly to the possibility that it is the character of the municipal setting and the patterning of citizens' attitudes toward local government that are different from what the broader participation literature would lead us to expect.

This general interpretation can be tested more specifically through comparative analysis of citizen-initiated contacting and other modes of political participation. Verba and Nie's (1972) conclusion that particularized contacting differs from other modes of participation is based in part on their evidence that such contacting is the one activity not susceptible to explanation through the socioeconomic model: "In short, the standard socioeconomic model works very well for our overall measure of activity and for campaign and communal activity. It works less well—but quite well nevertheless—for voting. It does not work for particularized contacting" (1972: 135–36). This conclusion has already been challenged by evidence that general referent contacting does not differ from particularized contacting with respect to socioeconomic correlates. In addition, data from the Kansas City study show that socioeconomic variables do not fare much better at explaining a variety of other forms of participation in the urban setting than they do in accounting for contacting. Table 2-6 shows summary measures of association between each of the key socioeconomic variables and five types of political involvement in addition to contacting. These additional types of participation cover virtually all of the categories considered by

TABLE 2-6. *Socioeconomic Variables and Six Types of Political Participation*

Type of Participation*	Income Gamma	r†	Education Gamma	r†
Vote regularly in local elections	.15	.17	.19	.20
Voted in last local election	.20	.15	.20	.14
Attend political meetings	.19	.14	.30	.19
Group membership	.11	.08	.22	.13
Work with neighbors on local problems	.17	.13	.19	.13
Contact local official	.11	.08	.12	.09

*Specific items were worded as follows: What about local elections generally—do you always vote in those, do you sometimes miss one, or do you rarely vote, or do you never vote? This past August there was an election in Kansas City. Did you vote in that election? In the past three or four years have you attended any political meetings like fund raisers or rallies or meetings with candidates? Are you a member of any group or organization in this community that works to solve community problems? Have you ever worked with your neighbors or other people in this community to do something about a local problem? In the past year, have you contacted any city government official or agency about any local problem or issue?

†All r values are significant at less than .01 level.

Verba and Nie, including voting (two items on voting in local elections), campaign activity (one item on attending political meetings), and communal activity (an item on group membership and one on working with neighbors to solve local problems). As Table 2-6 shows, income is the weaker of the two predictor variables for virtually all of these forms of participation. The education variable, however, also has surprisingly limited predictive power for these various forms of political participation.

In sum, this study has found that citizen-initiated contacting, as several other analysts have argued (Verba and Nie, 1972; Jones et al., 1977), is not susceptible to explanation by the socioeconomic model. But, this is not grounds for the conclusion that contacting (either overall or particularized) is distinctive from other modes of political participation. The socioeconomic model is also weak in accounting for a variety of other forms of participation *in the urban context*.

The relative weakness of the socioeconomic model in explaining contacting in Kansas City contrasts with findings of a strong relationship between SES and contacting in Wichita (Sharp, 1982). Kansas City has a well-established central complaints unit, but Wichita does not. Such a unit may contribute to the diffusion of political information relevant to the contacting process and to perceptions that city hall is accessible. The finding that, in Kansas City, political awareness variables are less strongly associated with SES than might normally be expected is consistent with the conjecture that a central complaints unit can have a leveling effect on political awareness (Vedlitz, Dyer, and Durand, 1980: 65); and this leveling effect would simultaneously weaken the ability of socioeconomic variables to explain contacting behavior.

The weakness of the socioeconomic model, as noted above, has implications for the need-awareness model as well. Hence it is time for an exploration of patterns of contacting in Kansas City vis-à-vis the need-awareness model, with particular attention to the fact that political awareness is at best (that is, with "knowledge of officials" as the measure) only moderately associated with social status.

Contacting and the Need-Awareness Model

In their study of contacting in Detroit, Jones and colleagues (1977) found a parabolic pattern of contacting propensity. That is, contacting was greatest in areas at the middle range of social well-being (roughly, an areal equivalent of socioeconomic status). This pattern is accounted for by a model stipulating that contacting is a function of both need and awareness. It is further assumed that need for government service is inversely associated with social well-being whereas awareness of government is positively associated with social well-being. Because sufficient levels of both need and awareness are required for heightened contacting propensity according to this model, contacting should be highest in middle social well-being areas (see Chapter 1).

Although the need-awareness model is designed to account for differential contacting propensity across areal units, the model might be applicable to individual behavior as well. The components of the model (awareness and need) can readily be treated as individual characteristics, especially if the need component is conceptualized as perceived need rather than objective neighborhood need. The relationship between objective and perceived need is, of course, an interesting question in itself, and it will be addressed in Chapter 3. Here, the intent is to apply the need-awareness model to individual contacting behavior. Perceived need, rather than objective neighborhood need, is used at this point because it is more directly relevant to explanation at the individual level. Whatever objective neighborhood conditions may be, they will be relevant to motivating individual contacts only to the extent that the individual perceives them as constituting problems worthy of government attention.

As we have seen, only one of the three political awareness variables—knowledge of government officials—is even moderately associated with socioeconomic status, and that variable is much less strongly associated with contacting than would be expected on the basis of the socioeconomic model. The need-awareness model, unlike the socioeconomic model, provides a reason for expecting this—it stipulates that awareness is only part of the picture. Awareness must be coupled with need before either has a significant effect on propensity to contact government officials. If the need-awareness model were to apply to individual contacting propensity in Kansas City, it would therefore provide at least one additional avenue for understanding the failure of the socioeconomic model—that model's failure to include need.

The parabolic pattern of contacting propensity that the need-awareness model predicts (and that Jones and colleagues found in Detroit) is not mirrored in the individual-level data from Kansas City. Relationships between SES variables and contacting are

Patterns of Contacting

weak, but not because the positive, linear associations hypothesized under the socioeconomic model are replaced by curvilinear patterns in the data. Although a traditional test for curvilinearity cannot be applied because we are dealing with a dummy dependent variable and ordinal independent variables, Figures 2-1 and 2-2 present contacting propensity across education and income categories (without the major collapsing of

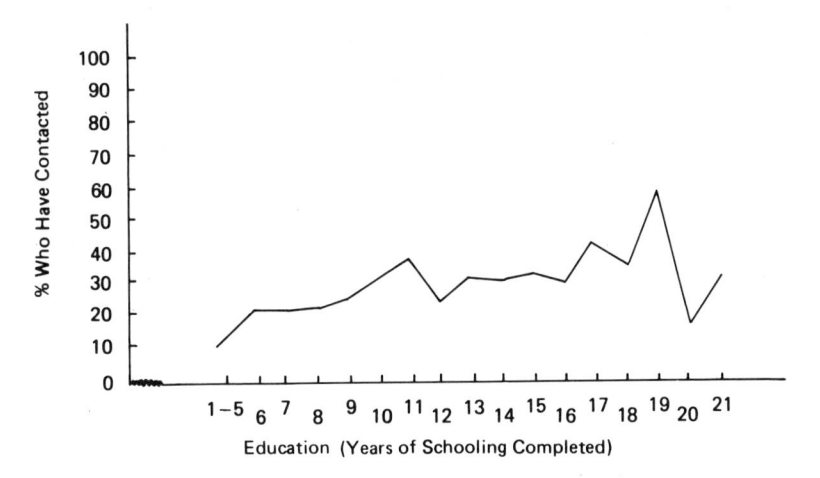

FIGURE 2-1. *Education and Contacting*

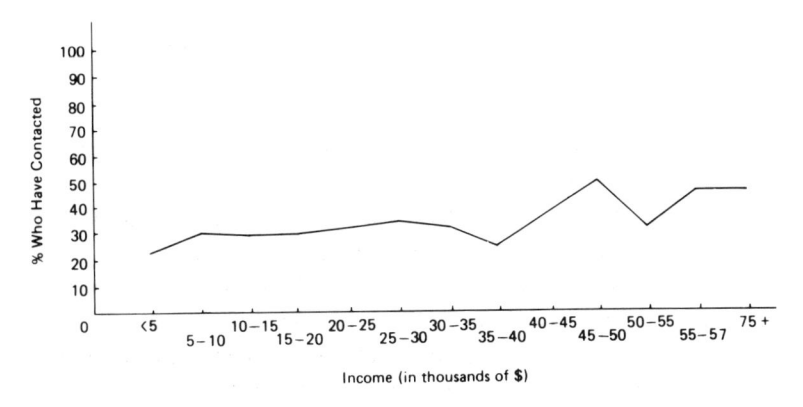

FIGURE 2-2. *Income and Contacting*

categories that was useful for a compact presentation in Table 2-1). Although there is an unexpected drop in contacting propensity at the high end of the education scale, neither of these figures comes close to approximating the downward opening parabola that the need-awareness model predicts.

For these reasons, the need-awareness model, like the socioeconomic model, appears to be an unsuitable explanation of contacting behavior, at least at the individual level. It is important to consider why this model is not suitable.

On the left (panel A) of Figure 2-3 is the original need-awareness model and the pattern of contacting that it predicts. On the right (panel B) is a schematic drawing of what we have already learned about political awareness and socioeconomic status—at best (with the "knowledge of government" variable representing awareness), there is a moderate association with socioeconomic status, particularly the education variable.

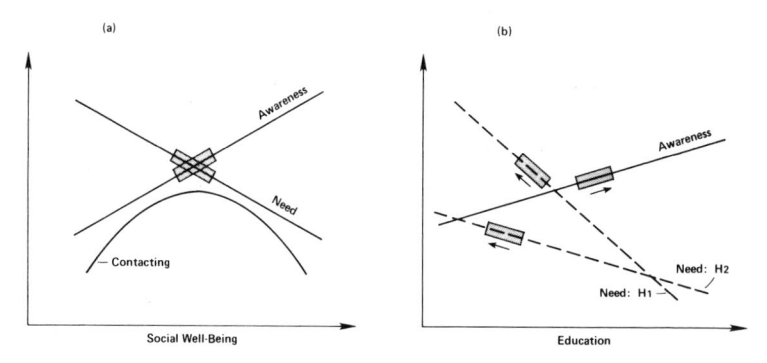

FIGURE 2-3. *The Need-Awareness Model: Possible Scenarios*

Figure 2-3B also shows that whether need and awareness work together to generate the pattern of contacting suggested in the original need-awareness model depends in part on the relationship of the need variable to education. It is also, however, a matter of thresholds. The original model posits that sufficient levels of both need and awareness are necessary to motivate contacting behavior, and it is assumed that in the middle range of

Patterns of Contacting

social well-being, there will be sufficient levels of both. Even if need shows a strong inverse relationship with education, however, as the Jones model suggests (see Need: H1 in Figure 2-3B), there may be no subgroup for which a "sufficient" level of need is matched with a "sufficient" level of awareness to raise contacting propensity significantly from a low-level norm for the population as a whole. This would be the case if, as in Figure 2-3B, "sufficient" levels of need and awareness are the threshold levels indicated in boxed zones. The education group at the intersection of awareness and need (H1) would be just below the required thresholds of both need and awareness. The next higher education group might reach the threshold for awareness, but for that group need is considerably below the threshold; meanwhile, less-educated groups would meet the need threshold but miss the awareness threshold. Furthermore, if need is less strongly associated with socioeconomic status than the model suggests (see Need: H2 in Figure 2-3B), no education grouping comes close to meeting both threshold levels for heightened contacting propensity.

To examine this issue empirically, a measure of perceived need was constructed from a set of fourteen potential problem items such as streets flooding when it storms, houses that are unsafe, and streets that are in poor repair.[3] For each item, the respondent was asked: Is this a "big problem," "somewhat of a problem," or "not a problem at all" in your neighborhood? The need variable used here is a count of the number of items that the respondent saw as big problems. Overall, 53 percent reported no big problems in their neighborhood, another 23 percent reported only one big problem, 16 percent saw two or three items as big problems, and the remaining 8 percent reported more than three problems.

As Table 2-7 shows, the perceived need variable is a comparatively good predictor of contacting. Need is in fact a stronger predictor than any other variable considered so far except political efficacy. This is an important finding, and one to which I will return later.

Somewhat surprisingly, however, need is not as strongly associ-

TABLE 2-7. *Perceived Need and Contacting (percentages)*

Contacted Local Official	Level of Perceived Need			
	Lowest (0 Problems)	Low (1 Problem)	Moderate (2–3 Problems)	High (4+ Problems)
Yes	21	30	38	51
No	79	70	62	49
	100	100	100	100
(N)	(1,126)	(498)	(335)	(189)

Gamma = .34
Kendall's Tau$_b$ = .19
Pearson's r = .21   Sig. < .01

ated with socioeconomic status as might be expected. Need is only modestly associated with income (gamma = −.14; r = −.16) and with education (gamma = −.11; r = −.13). Although both are inverse relationships as expected, both are surprisingly weak.

Before proceeding, it is important to consider whether the results just reported are merely an artifact of a less-than-optimal perceived need measure. The measure is based only on citizens' ratings of certain items as "big problems" in their neighborhood. Would the results be different if perceived "moderate problems" were also included? This possibility can be tested by constructing an alternative measure of perceived need that sums responses to the fourteen potential problem items, with "big problem" responses coded as 2 and "moderate problem" responses coded as 1; responses of "not a problem at all" are coded 0. This measure yields a distribution in which 14 percent of respondents have a summary score of 0, 28 percent score 1 or 2, 29 percent score 3 to 5, 20 percent score 6 to 10, and only 9 percent have a score greater than 10 (the highest possible score is 28). This measure of perceived need behaves much like the original measure. Again, perceived need is much less strongly associated with education (gamma = −.06; r = −.10) or with income (gamma = −.09; r = −.14) than the need-awareness model might lead us to expect; indeed, the relationships are minimized when this alternative measure of perceived need is used. The relationship between the alternative measure of perceived need and contacting is identical to that between the original perceived need measure and contacting (gamma = .34; r = .24).

It is also possible that the weak relationships between perceived need and both income and education arise because the perceived need measure aggregates responses across fourteen potential problem items that may be differentially important to better-off and less-well-off respondents. For example, traffic and street quality problems may be more important to upper-status residents and rundown housing a more salient problem for lower-status residents. The weakness of the perceived need–SES relationships then may be a result of aggregating across such offsetting items.

An examination of relationships between individual potential problem items and SES measures suggests that SES-perceived problem relationships are not uniform across the problem items, but that there is not a pattern of truly offsetting relationships. Focusing on relationships with education, for example, we find that only the traffic problems item shows a significant positive relationship (gamma = .13; r = .07). Six of the fourteen items (flooding, street repair, garbage collection, street lighting, bus service, and animal control) are negligibly related to education (gammas with absolute values of less than .04). The remaining seven items show modest, negative associations with education, just as the composite perceived need measure does. The strongest of these are the relationships between rat or pest problems and education (gamma = −0.20; r = −.15) and between vacant building problems and education (gamma = −0.20; r = −.10).

In short, there is no evidence here that strong positive associations between some problems and SES are being offset by strong negative associations between other problems and SES. All but one of the items show either negligible associations or associations in the same direction and of the same order of magnitude as the composite measure. We therefore return to the conclusion reached before this treatment of measurement issues—that income and education are surprisingly weak predictors of perceived need.

As noted above, this conclusion will have consequences for the need-awareness model outlined by Jones and colleagues. This is shown graphically in Figure 2-4, which charts average knowledge (awareness) and average need scores for each education grouping. The pattern most closely approximates the schema in Figure 2-3B with Need: H2. We do not know, of course, what the threshold levels of need and knowledge are. For purposes of discussion, however, let us assume that the overall average scores for need and awareness are the threshold points. These are indicated in Figure 2-4.

No socioeconomic subgroup (defined on the basis of education) is substantially above average on both need and awareness. The two groups that come closest are those with fifteen and those with seventeen years of schooling. Both are noticeably above average on knowledge of government officials, and both are just about at the average for need.

A comparison of Figure 2-4 with Figure 2-2 shows that there are three progressive peaks of contacting propensity (Figure 2-2), but these do not fully correspond with what a need-awareness model interpretation of Figure 2-4 would suggest. Although one of the peaks of contacting propensity occurs at seventeen years of schooling (consistent with expectations), those with fifteen years of schooling are not particularly prone to contact, as Figure 2-4 suggests they might be. Furthermore, the most contact-prone group of all—those with nineteen years of education—is extremely high on knowledge of government officials but among the lowest on need.

It is possible, of course, that the appropriate thresholds have not been identified in Figure 2-4. This is, in fact, the major problem with the need-awareness model. It is not enough to posit

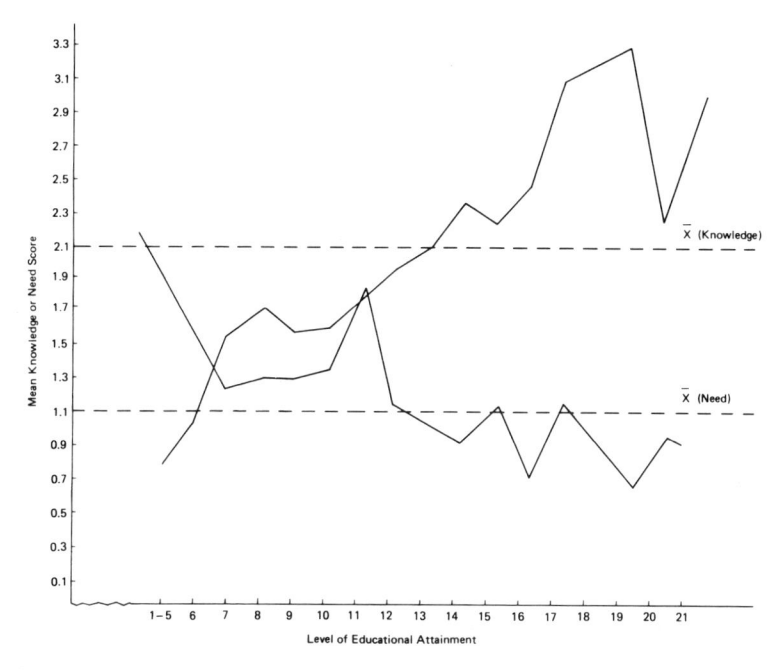

FIGURE 2-4. *Average Need and Knowledge (Awareness) Levels, by Education Group*

that there will be a significant interaction effect between need and awareness when "sufficient" levels of both are present. We need to know what these threshold levels of sufficiency are, and there is nothing so far to suggest how these might be established.

Indeed, it is possible that there is no single threshold level of either need or awareness, applicable across all socioeconomic groups. Rather, it may be that what are unusual levels of political awareness and need for a lower-status individual would not be unusual for a higher-status individual; exceeding these "usual" levels may be required for political mobilization. This logic has been applied in the study of international conflict, in which the concept of a "normal relations range" has been developed (Azar, 1978), recognizing that an unusual level of conflictual communication between one pair of nation-states may not be unusual for another pair. For a pair of normally very conflictual nations, diplomatic communications or ongoing events that might be highly provocative for a normally less conflictual pair of nations would be well within the normal relations range and therefore unlikely to engender mobilization.

If this logic of normal ranges were applied to the phenomenon at hand, contacting propensity would be viewed as contingent upon the threshold levels of need and awareness for various socioeconomic subgroups and the likelihood that individuals in a given socioeconomic group will exceed these threshold levels. Unfortunately, the need-awareness model does not incorporate such a contingent view of mobilization for contacting, nor have normal ranges of political awareness and perceived need been empirically established.

In sum, the full need-awareness model does not provide a useful explanation of individual contacting propensity in Kansas City, in part because virtually no SES subgroup can be identified as clearly exceeding threshold levels of both need and awareness. But the need-awareness model does make an important contribution to the explanation of contacting behavior: it offers need for government services as an important explanatory factor, and this is empirically substantiated in the Kansas City data.

Summary

Anaylsis of individual contacting behavior has so far shown that neither the standard socioeconomic model nor the need-awareness model fares very well. Each model, however, does contribute to explanation of this form of demand-making in the urban context. Although the relationship is weak, contacting is linked to educational attainment; and, although it does not function as a mediating variable in the way that the standard SES model suggests, the individual's sense of efficacy is a significant predictor of contacting. Finally, perceived need is a relatively important predictor of contacting.

Taken together, however, these three explanatory variables leave considerable unexplained variation in contacting propensity. To summarize, the contacting variable was regressed on these three variables. The results are shown in Table 2-8. Again, we see that efficacy and need are the more important of the explanatory factors; education is less important. But we are far from a full understanding of contacting propensity. The regression model presented in Table 2-8 results in a multiple R of .28, suggesting a promising start, but the need remains to press further for an understanding of the factors generating citizen demands.

If something is missing from this explanation, it may well be the neighborhood context within which demand-making takes place. The focus so far on individual characteristics is the natural result of efforts to explain individual differences in contacting—that is, why do some citizens engage in this form of demand-making while others do not? Characteristics of the neighborhood may be important as well. Many urban services are delivered to neighborhoods rather than to individuals (for example, allocation of police officers to beats and placement and maintenance of area parks); and many of the problems of urban life are spatially allocated as well (Jones, 1980). Hence the circumstances that may engender demand-making are at least to some extent shared by residents of urban neighborhoods; and, as we have already seen, most citizens who report having made a contact with local government perceive that they requested something of relevance to their community, not just to themselves.

All of this suggests the importance of examining characteristics

TABLE 2-8. *Explaining Contacting: Multiple Regression Results**

Contact	= 1.002 + 0.052 Efficacy + 0.038 Need + 0.012 Education
Standard error	(.006) (.006) (.003)
Multiple R	= .280
Adjusted R^2	= .007
(N)	= 2,106

*Unstandardized regression coefficients are presented.

of the neighborhood context to understand individual demand-making more fully. The following chapter takes up this task, again using both the socioeconomic model and the need-awareness model as springboards for such a contextual analysis.

NOTES TO CHAPTER 2

1. Seligson (1980) also summarizes a variety of criticisms of the SRC efficacy scale and the subjective competence measure used by Almond and Verba (1963). These include item ambiguity, strong potential for social desirability response set or acquiescence response set, temporal instability and unreliability, and, in the case of the hypothetical situations posed in the subjective competence measure, imposition of a researcher-defined scenario that may not be relevant for the respondent. He also notes George Balch's (1974) argument that a sense of efficacy is in relation to a particular level of government or government institution.
2. Respondents were asked to name the mayor, the city manager, their district council member, and any other council member without benefit of a list of names to choose from. Awareness of the Action Center is included in the knowledge index because of the special relevance of this central complaints unit for citizen-initiated contacts. Respondents were asked if they had heard of Kansas City's Action Center. Because there are other, similar-sounding entities such as a media Action Line, those who responded affirmatively were asked what the Action Center is; only those who gave answers coded as correct by interviewers were treated as knowing about the Action Center.
3. The fourteen items are as follows: How about not having a park that is enjoyable? What about flooding when it storms? Houses that are rundown? Potholes or streets in bad repair? Not getting garbage picked up right? Houses that are not built to be safe? Mosquitoes, rats, or similar pests? Inadequate stop signs, traffic lights, or other traffic problems? Trash piles, junk, or weeds on people's property? Vacant buildings that are dangerous? Streets not lighted well enough? Stray dogs or other animal problems? Poor bus service? Weeds or high grass?

3

The Neighborhood Context for Demand-Making

☑ ☑ ☐
☑ ☐ ☐

So far, a variety of explanations of citizen demand-making have been pursued, but all from the perspective of an individual level of analysis. There are several good reasons for expanding this perspective to include neighborhood-level characteristics as possible explanatory variables. First, one of the two major models that has been introduced, the need-awareness model, was originally developed for neighborhood-level analysis. That model does not fare very well when applied at the individual level, as in Chapter 2. Vedlitz, Dyer, and Durand (1980) were also unable to find evidence for the need-awareness model in their analysis of individual contacting behavior in Dallas and Houston. They conclude that this may be because the model is applicable at the aggregate, neighborhood level, but it is not appropriate for individual behavior. But we need not choose between a pure individual-level analysis and a pure aggregate-level analysis. It may be possible to synthesize elements of the need-awareness model with explanations more appropriate at the individual level of analysis by incorporating neighborhood need and awareness as contextual variables.

Second, a strong line of research shows that a variety of forms of political activity are influenced by social context as well as by individual attributes. R. Robert Huckfeldt summarizes this line of research as follows: "Political activity seldom occurs in individual isolation; as a result, the social context is an important determinant of the extent to which individuals participate in politics. Individual characteristics, attributes, and personality factors do not entirely determine the extent of individual political activity. People also respond to political events, cues, and opportunities which are specific to a given environment" (1979: 579).

Contacting behavior has been characterized as a very instrumental, individualistic mode of political assertion (Verba and Nie, 1972; Thomas, 1982), and Huckfeldt (1979: 582) argues that "acts such as those should be less subject to contextual influence." If contacting merits the individualistic characterization that it is often given, we should expect to find few neighborhood contextual effects on contacting behavior. If, on the other hand, we do find contextual effects, we will have evidence of the neighborhood social conditions that help to mobilize citizens for demand-making.

In addition, a contextual analysis may help us to further understand the failure of the socioeconomic model to account for contacting. If contextual factors are relatively powerful, a contingency version of the socioeconomic model may be most appropriate. That is, the extent to which individuals' socioeconomic attributes are linked to contacting may depend upon the socioeconomic composition of the neighborhood in which the individual is located.

Three aspects of the neighborhood context will be considered in this chapter: its socioeconomic composition, the level of objective need for government services, and the character of neighborhood organizations. With respect to the first of these, we will explore the possibility that the connection between an individual's social status (particularly, level of educational attainment) and contacting propensity is contingent upon the social milieu in which one is located.

Second, the analysis turns to levels of objective need in the neighborhood. As the preceding chapter shows, the individual's perception of need for government services is one of the most important predictors of contacting behavior. The link between objective need and perceived need has yet to be explored, however. I will examine the extent to which individual perceptions of need are a function of objective conditions in the neighborhood and explore other sources of perceived need.

Finally, neighborhood organizations may be expected to have an impact on the citizen's propensity to register demands with city government, particularly by providing avenues of access to city government beyond those available to individual citizens. The final section of this chapter documents the role of neighborhood organizations in the demand-making process.

Neighborhood Socioeconomic Context

Individual socioeconomic attributes such as education and income level are surprisingly weakly related to contacting behavior, as was demonstrated in Chapter 2. Education shows a stronger association than income, but the association is so weak as to call into question the entire socioeconomic model as an explanation of contacting.

Individuals' propensity to engage in political acts, however, is not necessarily a function only of their socioeconomic status. The social milieu in which they are located may have an important mediating effect. This possibility is consistent with the logic of the socioeconomic model. As noted earlier, that model does not simply specify that higher-status citizens are more likely to participate in politics. It also posits that this pattern exists because higher-status citizens are more likely to develop the skills and attitudes that predispose one toward political involvement. Bettereducated individuals, for example, are viewed as having gone through a socialization process that includes exposure to those who are sophisticated about government processes, the inculcation of civic values, and the learning of relevant political information. These notions of exposure and socialization open up the possibility that individuals of lower social status might develop similar attitudes and skills if, through residential mobility or other means, they are exposed to upper-status social contexts.

An alternative hypothesis has also been offered concerning the effects of a discrepancy between one's own social status and the social context of the neighborhood. Building upon Lazarsfeld and associates' (1948) analysis of social cross-pressures, Huckfeldt argues that "the social context . . . is capable of discouraging as well as encouraging political participation" (1979: 581). This can be the case if lower-status individuals develop "feelings of political inferiority" in a higher-status setting or are excluded from neighborhood social settings in which they might have developed political skills and values. Huckfeldt found, for example, that the effect of neighborhood social context differs for individuals of different levels of educational attainment: "Higher status contexts are related to more active participation among high status respondents . . . the effect of higher status contexts is almost exactly the opposite among low status respondents; low educated individuals living in high education neighborhoods are over 20 percent less likely to work at getting people registered than low educated individuals living in low education neighborhoods" (1979: 582).

As Figure 3-1 shows, Huckfeldt's (1979) findings for participation in getting people registered to vote are, in part, replicated here for contacting behavior. Individuals with the highest level of educational attainment are more predisposed to contact officials if they live in high-education neighborhoods than if they live in a lower-education setting; the least well-educated individuals show the opposite pattern—their contacting propensity drops off sharply in the context of a high-education neighborhood. Those in the two mid-range categories of educational attainment (twelve years and thirteen to sixteen years) converge in the high-education neighborhood context at a moderate rate of contacting propensity.

Figure 3-1 also shows that for all levels of individual educational attainment, contacting is less in the neighborhoods of average educational attainment than in lower education neighborhoods. To the extent that neighborhood educational level

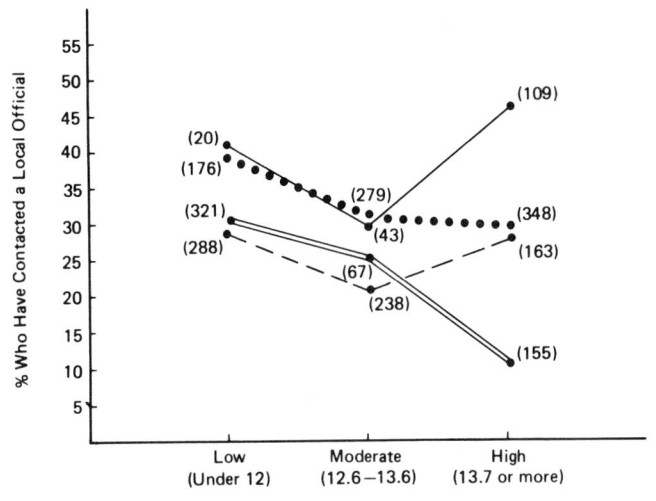

The Neighborhood Context

[Figure 3-1: Scatter/line plot. Y-axis: % Who Have Contacted a Local Official (5 to 55). X-axis: Mean Level of Educational Attainment in Neighborhood — Low (Under 12), Moderate (12.6–13.6), High (13.7 or more). Data points with Ns: (20), (176), (321), (288) at Low; (279), (43), (67), (238) at Moderate; (109), (348), (163), (155) at High.]

Individual Educational Attainment: Key
═══ Less than 12 years
--- 12 years
••• 13–16 years
——— 17–21 years

Conditional Gammas
Education and Contacting in:
Low Education Neighborhoods .10
Moderate Education Neighborhoods .17
High Education Neighborhoods .28

FIGURE 3-1. *Education, Contacting, and the Neighborhood Socioeconomic Context*

roughly points to the level of social well-being in the neighborhood, this pattern may be a manifestation of the importance of need—that is, there may be more cause for demand-making in the lowest-status neighborhoods than in the average-status neighborhoods.

Furthermore, the differences in contacting propensity across the different levels of individual educational attainment are relatively small in both low-education and moderate-education neighborhoods. It is only in the higher-education neighborhoods that contacting propensity by level of individual educational attainment diverges sharply—and in the direction that the socioeconomic model suggests. Figure 3-1 illustrates, then, that the socioeconomic model has some relevance in higher-status contexts that it does not have in other contexts. In higher-status contexts, better-educated individuals are in a propitious setting for political activation and less-educated individuals are apparently not politically mobilized by the social setting. In lower-status contexts, better-educated citizens are still the most likely to contact government officials. The differences are negligible, however, because the least-educated citizens show their highest levels of contacting propensity in these neighborhoods, where there is no marked discrepancy between their status and the neighborhood social context.

The evidence suggests that upward mobility in a residential location sense cannot necessarily be expected to enhance the political assertiveness of less-educated citizens. Rather, the evidence is consistent with Lazarsfeld and associates' (1948) conceptions of social cross-pressures as inhibitors to political participation, at least for individuals with lower social status.

In short, the neighborhood socioeconomic context does make a difference, but the difference is relatively subtle. This contextual analysis gives us a contingency perspective on the basic socioeconomic model, that is, it specifies one setting (high-education neighborhoods) where the socioeconomic model is most relevant for understanding differences in contacting propensity.

Even in that setting, however, the socioeconomic model is only a partial explanation of variation in contacting propensity. This may be because, as was shown in Chapter 2, the political attitudes and skills that are crucial intervening variables in the socioeconomic model are not necessarily important in predisposing citizens to make demands upon city government. Instead, perceived need is a more powerful predictor of contacting propensity. For this reason, objective, quality-of-life conditions in the neighborhood may be a more important part of the context for demand-making than neighborhood socioeconomic context.

Objective Need in the Neighborhood

Although there may be no consensus within the social sciences on the operational meaning of "quality of life," it is surely true that objective conditions that affect the quality of life vary tremendously across urban neighborhoods. Here, the focus is on a set of conditions that parallels the battery of survey items used to measure perceived need (within the limits of available data). Objective indicators of a variety of neighborhood conditions are derived from archival sources in city government, ratings by trained observers, and 1980 census data.

For example, the city's Department of Public Works has amassed data on storm sewer flooding problems in the city as of December 1982 and the costs to correct each problem site. After geo-coding this list to the twenty-four study neighborhoods and standardizing for the number of dwelling units in the neighborhood, we find that seven neighborhoods have no flooding problems, one needs repair work worth $298,000 per dwelling unit to correct flooding problems, and another—the predominantly Hispanic neighborhood on the city's west side—needs repair work worth $755,000 per dwelling unit.

The Department of Public Works also keeps records of rat sightings throughout the city, and all those reported from January through March 1983 were geo-coded to the study neighborhoods. These, too, are not equally distributed across the neighborhoods, even correcting for the number of dwelling units in the neighborhoods. Three neighborhoods had no rat sightings, thirteen had fewer than ten sightings per thousand dwelling units, and six (Valleydale, Dupree, Belton, Bluewood, Easterling, and Ivy Hill)[1] had more than twenty per thousand dwelling units.

A pair of trained observers was dispatched to rate street conditions, sidewalk conditions, the extent of high weeds, street litter, and junk objects or trash piles on property (that is, potential environmental code violations) at five randomly selected points within each study neighborhood. Pictoral scales developed at the

Urban Institute were used to rate street and litter conditions, a verbal descriptive scale was the basis for sidewalk ratings, and yes-no codings were used to indicate whether junk objects or high weeds were present at each of the sampled locations. Again, there was substantial variation across the neighborhoods. For example, in seven of the neighborhoods, high weeds were spotted in none of the five sampled sites; in three (Ivy Hill, Dupree, and Belton) high weeds were encountered at all five sites. In most of the neighborhoods, junk objects or trash piles were not evident at any of the sites; but in Bluewood, Ivy Hill, and Westview, such problems were evident in three of the five locations. Average ratings of street conditions ranged from 1.2 in West Park to 2.3 in Jackson, and average ratings of sidewalk conditions ranged from 1.0 in West Park, Wentworth, Clover Downs, Greenbriar, and Jackson to 3.0 in Belton and 3.2 in Ivy Hill. (A higher score indicates a more severe problem.)

Finally, as the discussion of study neighborhood selection showed (see Chapter 1), housing quality, at least as reflected in housing value, also varies considerably across these neighborhoods. The average value of owner-occupied housing, according to 1980 census data, ranges from $102,000 in the Robard neighborhood to $14,000 in Westview and Belton.

Even from this brief review of indicators of quality-of-life conditions, it is obvious that some neighborhoods emerge repeatedly as "problem" areas; others may show poorly on some indicators but not on others. To derive a single, composite measure of neighborhood objective conditions, or objective need, the eight objective indicators described above are combined into a single measure. The rating of each neighborhood on each of the eight individual indicators is transformed into a standard score (Z-score transformation) for standardized scaling across the eight measures. The overall measure of objective need is the sum of these standard scores for each neighborhood.[2] For the twenty-four study neighborhoods, this summary measure of objective need ranges from -7 (for the neighborhood with the least objective need) to +10 (for the neighborhood with the most objective need). In short, some Kansas Citians live in neighborhoods where objective conditions are problematic and others live in neighborhoods where conditions are good—a finding that would not surprise observers of the urban scene in America.

These differences in the neighborhood context—differences in objective need for government services—are what Jones and colleagues (1977) hypothesize to be critical to mobilization of citizens for demand-making. Others (Thomas, 1982; Sharp, 1984b) have argued that objective need mobilizes citizens for demand-making only to the extent that the need is recognized. The influence of objective need, in other words, is mediated by perceived need.

If objective need and perceived need showed a very strong association, this refinement would be relatively unimportant. Perceived need and objective need could be treated as proxy measures of each other, and objective need should be about as good a predictor of contacting propensity as is perceived need. Table 3-1 suggests that the situation is not that simple.

When neighborhood need is treated as an ecological variable, "attached" to the individual, a positive association between objective need in the neighborhood and the individual's level of perceived need emerges. Obviously, the sociospatial incidence of the objective conditions included in our measure of objective need can be small relative to the size of the neighborhood. For this reason, a one-on-one correspondence between perceived need and objective need would not be expected. Even with this caveat in mind, the association is still weaker than might be expected. Perceived need is clearly not purely a function of objective need. In the objectively "better-off" neighborhoods, about two-thirds of all respondents rated none of the fourteen items asked about as "big problems"; residents of neighborhoods with the worst objective conditions were less likely to cite no big problems, yet more than one-third of them named none of the items as big problems in the neighborhood. Furthermore, only about one-fifth of the

TABLE 3-1. *Perceived Need and Objective Need in the Neighborhood (percentages)*

	Objective Need Score for Neighborhood				
Percent of Respondents Who Perceive	←Lesser Need			Greater Need→	
	−4 or Less	−2.00 to −3.99	−1.99 to 0	0 to 3.99	More than 4.00
No big problems	64	61	51	51	35
Only one big problem	22	22	30	23	22
Two or three big problems	11	13	16	16	22
Four or more big problems	2	4	3	10	22
	99	100	100	100	101
(N)	(416)	(535)	(284)	(461)	(464)

Gamma = .29
Kendall's Tau$_b$ = .20
Pearson's r = .27   Sig. < .01

residents in the objectively most problem-ridden neighborhoods saw their neighborhood as high on need (that is, they identified more than three big problems).

Furthermore, as Table 3-2 shows, objective need does not show a positive, linear relationship with contacting propensity, as does

TABLE 3-2. *Objective Need and Contacting (percentages)*

	Objective Need Score for Neighborhood				
	←Lesser Need			Greater Need→	
Contacted a Local Official	−4 or Less	−2.00 to −3.99	−1.99 to 0	0 to 3.99	More than 4.00
Yes	30	27	24	30	28
No	70	73	76	70	72
	100	100	100	100	100

Gamma = .00
Kendall's Tau$_b$ = .00
Pearson's r = .01   Sig. = .40

the perceived need measure. Nor is there evidence of higher levels of contacting at some middle range of objective need, as the need-awareness model suggests. Instead, residents of neighborhoods at all levels of objective need are similar in their propensity to contact government officials with complaints or requests for service.

In short, objective need is not directly linked to demand-making. Whatever importance it has for demand-making is indirect, mediated by perceived need.

Yet Table 3-1 shows that the link between objective and perceived need is surprisingly modest, which suggests that objective need is only one among a variety of factors contributing to the perception of need. Since the latter is an important predictor of demand-making, it is worthwhile to probe more deeply for these other sources of perceived need. Such an analysis also makes clear why objective need and perceived need are only loosely coupled. It is to this task that we now turn.

Sources of Perceived Need: Objective Need versus Expectations

The measure of perceived need used here is based on citizens' perceptions of particular items as being "big problems" in the neighborhood. But what, after all, is a problem, other than a disjunction between the circumstances that one sees oneself as facing and the expectations one has about what circumstances should be? Problem recognition of any kind therefore has two dimensions: (1) an observational component, involving assessments of objective conditions; and (2) a value component, involving expectations about what objective conditions should be like. Individuals perceive problems whenever there is a discrepancy between these two components.

This definitional foray suggests two main approaches for explaining variation in perceived need. One approach, exemplified in the analysis thus far, looks to objective conditions for an explanation of differences in perceived need. From this perspective, perceived need should be higher among some urban residents than others because some face objectively poorer conditions than others. Another approach emphasizes variation in individuals' expectations and assumes that, even when objective conditions are more or less equal, individual perceptions of need will differ because of a range of factors that mold individual expectations.

The hypothesis that perceived need is primarily a function of the objective conditions one faces (objective need) would appear to be relatively straightforward. Yet as shown in Table 3-1, the link between perceived and objective need is not as strong as might have been expected. Other analysts have also noted a lack of correspondence between objective conditions and citizens' perceptions (see Stipak, 1980, for a thorough review). This lack of correspondence is viewed as especially troublesome, given the trend toward use of citizens' subjective evaluations as performance indicators for local government (Stipak, 1979).

The model to be pursued here suggests that objective conditions only partly account for perceived need because of prevailing differences in citizens' expectations. Unfortunately, there is little theory available to provide hypotheses about variation in citizens' expectations of this sort. To a large extent, political scientists have treated expectations concerning the quality of urban life in the manner that economists have treated the parallel concept of preferences. That is, expectations are assumed to exist, and they are presumed to be politically relevant insofar as they influence citizens' evaluations of urban services and demand-making. Research on patterns of citizens' expectations has been badly neglected, however. Apart from some descriptive work concerning the elements that constitute quality of life for urban residents (Campbell, Converse, and Rodgers, 1976), the character of citizens' expectations has gone largely unexplored.

Here, four types of hypotheses concerning citizens' expectations and perceived need will be examined: a "connoisseurship"

The Neighborhood Context   69

explanation, a "stakeholding" explanation, a "demand creation" explanation, and an equity explanation.

The "connoisseurship" explanation is derived from Hirschman's (1970) discussion of the "quality conscious consumer." Hirschman argues that "a given deterioration in quality will inflict very different losses . . . on different customers; someone who had a very high consumer surplus before deterioration precisely because he is a connoisseur and would be willing to pay, say, twice the actual price . . . may drop out as a customer as soon as quality deteriorates" (1970: 48–49).

Although Hirschman's argument is framed in terms of "customers" of "articles," the same logic may be applied to citizens' expectations about conditions in their neighborhood. Those who are "connoisseurs" of these neighborhood conditions are particularly sensitive to deteriorations in their quality. They have, in other words, higher expectation levels and would presumably be more conscious of problems with these aspects of neighborhood condition.

But who are the connoisseurs? The term itself suggests that considerations of socioeconomic status may be at work. Higher-status citizens, in short, may have a view of what their neigh-

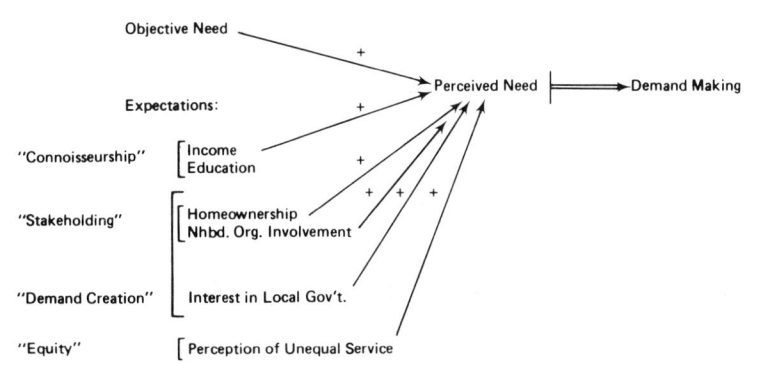

FIGURE 3-2. *Objective Need, Expectations, and Perceived Need: Hypotheses*

borhood should be like to be consistent with their status, and deviations might not be tolerated, even though the deviations represent less severe problems than those existing in lower-class neighborhoods.

This hypothesis of the "choosy" upper-class resident differs from existing interpretations of differences among social classes in the types of urban services considered important. There is evidence that lower-status citizens are most interested in social services, that in working-class communities housekeeping services predominate, and that upper-class citizens are most interested in "amenities" services (Lovrich, 1974; Adrian and Williams, 1963). Based on this and his own Cincinnati data, Thomas (1982) offers the conclusion that the relationship between socioeconomic status and perceived need depends upon the category of need at issue. If higher-status citizens appear to be more interested in amenities issues (such as parks) and less interested in basic service matters (such as dilapidated buildings) than are lower-status citizens, it may be because higher-status citizens have had their basic service needs met. One can afford to be concerned about amenities if there are neither crumbling streets nor chronic rat sightings in the neighborhood. To determine what expectations are, we need to examine how citizens' perceptions of need vary whenever objective conditions are more or less equal. The hypothesis of the upper-class urban resident as "connoisseur" suggests that, confronting objectively similar neighborhood conditions, higher-status residents will have a greater level of problem perception than will lower-status residents because the former have higher expectations.

This first hypothesis treats expectation levels in much the way that economists use the concept of tastes; it presumes that differing expectations concerning the quality of life in one's neighborhood are lifestyle considerations, intimately bound up with one's social status. From a slightly different perspective, variations in expectations about neighborhood conditions may be keyed to one's stake in the neighborhood. From this perspective, it is not one's social status but one's investment in the neighborhood that is the key to what one expects for the neighborhood. There are a variety of potential manifestations of stakeholding, but clearly one of the most significant should be homeownership, for it represents a distinct financial investment in the neighborhood. Membership in a community organization is another indicator of stakeholding, reflecting social investment and possibly psychological involvement in the neighborhood. As described below, membership in a community organization might be hypothesized to heighten citizens' expectations for reasons other than the stakeholding explanation offered here. For the moment, however, the stakeholding explanation yields a pair of additional hypotheses: objective conditions being equal, homeowners will have higher levels of perceived need than will nonowners; and community group members will have higher levels of perceived need than will nonmembers.

From yet another perspective, it can be argued that what people expect from government is contingent upon what they have been told they can expect. Expectations and the demands that they foster do not reflect inherent personality characteristics, according to this argument; rather, they are a socially constructed reality. Michael Lipsky, for example, argues that "overt expressions of demand for services tend to be more responsive to changes in the perceived availability of services than in changes in the underlying conditions that are commonly supposed to affect demand. In other words, perceived availability of service 'pulls' demand, not the other way around" (1980: 35).

In short, by signaling that certain problem-solving capacities are available and legitimate for citizens to call upon, governments can, in effect, create their own demand. This occurs because expectations have been raised, not because of change in the objective conditions that citizens face. This notion of heightened expectations emanating from "supply" signals is consistent with the growing literature on "bureaucratic demand creation" (Milward, 1980; Wildavsky, 1979).

The demand-creation argument outlined above, however, does not, in itself, provide hypotheses about whose expectations are more likely to be heightened. Presumably, all citizens are exposed to the demand-inducing trends to which the argument points. But citizens are unlikely to be equally exposed. Interest in local government, for example, may have a bearing on exposure. Attentive publics should know what local government is offering and may be familiar with what the concept of professionalized urban government supposedly means. Meanwhile, those who are uninterested in local government may be relatively immune to the expectation-enhancing forces outlined above. This logic yields the following hypothesis: objective conditions being equal, level of perceived need should be a positive function of the citizen's general interest in municipal government.

Neighborhood organizations are also important from the expectation-inducement perspective. Yates (1977) is one among many who note the interest aggregation and articulation functions of neighborhood organizations. They are, in his terms, "foot soldiers" in the "street fighting pluralism" that characterizes urban politics. This means that citizens involved in such neighborhood groups may receive more exposure to discussions of neighborhood problems, information about local government programs, and the like than citizens who are not involved. Furthermore, many cities have come to rely on neighborhood organizations for a variety of functions ranging from Community Development Block Grant project development to basic service coproduction. Neighborhood organizations, in other words, are a key to city government's outreach efforts. As such, they can play a role in the expectation-enhancement process outlined above. This provides another logical support for the hypothesis, set forth above, that objective conditions being equal, community group members will have higher levels of perceived need than will nonmembers. There, the hypothesis was grounded in a stakeholding explanation; here, the same hypothesis is derived from an expectation-inducement perspective.

Finally, the concept of relative deprivation offers yet another building block for linking perceived need to expectations. Individuals make a variety of comparisons between their own lot and that of others—comparisons that may yield findings of inequality. Although we are often reminded that inequality is not the same as inequity (Lineberry, 1977; Rich, 1982b: 5), perceived inequalities provide strong grounds for the development of a sense of inequity, particularly if there is no public ethic justifying the particular inequalities that are observed. This is likely to be the case with respect to urban services, particularly in reformed cities, because of the ethic of equal access to such services that is incorporated in the reform tradition. The citizen who believes that there are smoother streets, nicer parks, and better garbage collection in other neighborhoods is unlikely to have patience with "bureaucratic decision rule" explanations that justify such inequalities on the grounds of technical considerations.

Much of the research on inequalities and relative deprivation focuses on the political behaviors resulting from inequalities in wealth. In particular, there is considerable attention to the linkage between social inequality and political instability. Here, the focus is slightly different. Perceived inequality in urban government's treatment of neighborhoods is hypothesized to be another in a set of factors influencing perceived need for service. Objective conditions being equal, perceived inequality should be associated with higher levels of perceived need, again because of an expectation dynamic. Beliefs that other neighborhoods receive more or better services than one's own would, according to this hypothesis, heighten expectations about what one should be getting in one's own neighborhood.

To summarize, the foregoing section argues that variation in perceived need that is not explained by objective conditions reflects the expectations side of problem perception. From the perspectives of connoisseurship, stakeholding, demand creation, and relative deprivation, five hypotheses having to do with the expectation side of perceived need are derived. Objective neighborhood conditions being equal: (1) higher-status residents will have a greater level of perceived need than will lower-status residents; (2) homeownership should be positively associated with perceived need; (3) group membership should be positively associated with perceived need; (4) interest in city government should be positively associated with perceived need; and (5) perceived inequality in urban service delivery should be positively associated with perceived need.

To test these hypotheses, perceived need, income, and education variables were used, along with the composite objective need measure derived from measures of neighborhood conditions (see above). Group membership was measured by a yes-no survey item asking, Are you a member of any group or organization in this community that works to solve community problems? Homeownership status was also determined from a single survey item, with those who own or are buying their homes distinguished from renters, those in institutional housing, and those with other arrangements. Interest in city government was based on a trichotomous survey item asking, How interested would you say you are in the operations of city government? Response categories are "very interested," "somewhat interested," and "not at all interested."

The perceived inequity variable that is important from a relative deprivation perspective was based on a survey item asking, Compared to other neighborhoods in Kansas City, do you believe the quality of city services in your neighborhood is better, about the same, or worse? Those responding "about the same" were coded as 0, those responding "worse" were coded at +1, and those responding that the quality of services in their neighborhood is actually "better" than others were coded as −1. The logic of the coding specifies this as a measure of perception of inequality in which one's own neighborhood is on the short end of the stick. Those who believe their neighborhood is favored over others do perceive inequalities, but not inequalities that put them at a disadvantage.

Figure 3-3 presents the zero-order correlation between objective need and perceived need and partial correlations of all other variables with perceived need, controlling for objective need.[3]

The Neighborhood Context

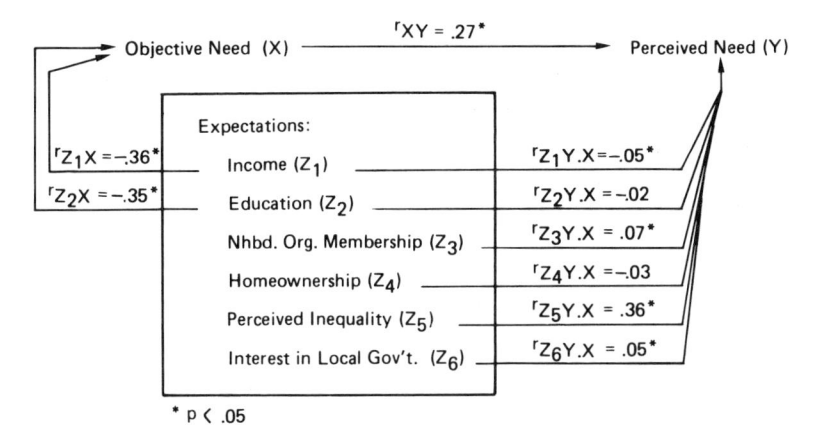

```
                          rXY = .27*
    ┌──► Objective Need (X) ─────────────► Perceived Need (Y)
    │                                              ▲
    │    ┌─────────────────────────────────────┐   │
    │    │  Expectations:                      │   │
 rZ₁X=-.36*│   Income (Z₁)         rZ₁Y.X = -.05*│
 rZ₂X=-.35*│   Education (Z₂)      rZ₂Y.X = -.02 │
         │   Nhbd. Org. Membership (Z₃)  rZ₃Y.X = .07*│
         │   Homeownership (Z₄)  rZ₄Y.X = -.03│
         │   Perceived Inequality (Z₅)  rZ₅Y.X = .36*│
         │   Interest in Local Gov't. (Z₆)  rZ₆Y.X = .05*│
         └─────────────────────────────────────┘

    * p < .05
```

FIGURE 3-3. *Objective Need, Expectations, and Perceived Need: Results*

This analytical approach is consistent with the logic of the hypothesis development, which specifies that variation in perceived need that is not explained by objective need is accounted for by factors related to expectations.

As in Table 3-1, there is a modest relationship between objective need and perceived need, but the link is not as strong as one might expect. Measurement problems may be, in part, responsible for this weakness. I will return to this possibility below. For the moment, the data show that citizens are not completely insensitive to objective conditions in their neighborhood, but that variation in objective conditions is only a part of the context for development of differing perceptions of need.

There is no support for the hypotheses derived from connoisseurship, stakeholding, and demand-creation perspectives. Only the perceived inequality hypothesis is supported. In fact, the partial correlation between perceived inequality and perceived need is the largest coefficient in Figure 3-3. Objective conditions being equal, perceived need is clearly associated with beliefs that other neighborhoods are better served.

It may also be useful to consider evidence of the relative

importance of each of the explanatory variables controlling for the effects of all others. Results of a multiple correlation analysis are presented in Table 3-3. The initial findings are replicated here. Again, the only significant predictors of perceived need are objective need and perceived inequality, and the latter is more important than the former.

TABLE 3-3. *Results of Regression of Perceived Need on Hypothesized Determinants*

Variable	b	Beta	Standard Error	F
Objective need	.007	.178	.012	38.285
Equality	1.668	.350	.127	172.265
Education	−.011	−.018	.012	0.340
Income	−.025	−.035	.022	1.313
Group membership	.172	.038	.122	1.994
Homeownership	−.134	−.032	.116	1.342
Interest	.106	.033	.086	1.517

Multiple $R = .44$
$R^2 = .19$
$N = 1190$

The disappointing performance of the neighborhood organization membership variable is perhaps especially surprising, given that a link between that variable and perceived need is hypothesized on two grounds—a stakeholding perspective and a demand-creation perspective. The likely problem here is the simplifying assumption that these organizations are all of a kind, when in fact they are not. Some of these organizations are intensely involved in the politics of urban service delivery, bring in guest speakers from city government, and have leaders that can help to raise residents' expectations of government by articulating what is available at city hall and the importance of making demands so that the neighborhood gets its share. Other neighborhood organizations are preoccupied with activities relatively far removed from the "street fighting pluralism" that Yates (1977) describes. Still others are virtually nonexistent shells.

In sum, the negligible relationship found here between organization membership and perceived need should not be interpreted as conclusive evidence that such organizations have absolutely no bearing on citizens' expectations of government. The results simply indicate that membership in and of itself does not necessarily expose citizens to expectation-enhancing forces. The nature and extent of the influence of neighborhood organizations on expectations and demand-making are likely to be contingent upon the characteristics of the organization. Exploration of these characteristics, using richer, more qualitative data, is the task of the final section of this chapter.

A comment on the socioeconomic variables is also in order. The hypothesis that these variables should be positively linked with perceived need derives from a connoisseurship explanation of the "choosy," quality-conscious, upper-status resident. Although this hypothesis of a direct link between socioeconomic status and perceived need is not supported, socioeconomic status is indirectly related to perceived need, via objective need. Specifically, there are relatively strong, negative associations between objective need and both income and education (r's of $-.36$ and $-.35$ respectively). This should not be surprising to any observer of the urban scene. As Richard Rich notes: "A tour of any city's neighborhoods will reveal marked, often startling differences in the physical characteristics and apparent quality of life in different areas. . . . Such a large proportion of goods and services are privately purchased in the United States that the basic quality of life in a neighborhood is necessarily intimately related to residents' personal income" (1982a: 2). Rich also argues that these differences in quality of life across urban neighborhoods surely reflect differences in the quality of public services received as well; but that is not the issue here. Instead, we note only that lower-income and less-educated citizens are more likely to live in neighborhoods with higher objective need; and objective need, in turn, shows a moderate, positive association with perceived need.

As noted above, the relative weakness of objective conditions in accounting for perceived need is consistent with a body of research on the general lack of correspondence between subjective measures (such as perceived need) and parallel measures of objective conditions (Stipak, 1980). Stipak offers several explanations for this lack of correspondence. One of these, a knowledgeability explanation, treats the lack of correspondence as a matter of measurement error, arising because survey respondents are sometimes asked about phenomena about which they have relatively little information. As Brian Stipak concludes: "the accuracy of citizen perceptions almost certainly decreases rapidly as the objective conditions or service characteristics become less specific, tangible, and more removed from the citizens' immediate environment" (1980: 17).

If we examine some of the potential problem items incorporated in the perceived need index and parallel measures of objective conditions, we find (see Table 3-4) that the link between subjective and objective measures is stronger in some areas than others. The data in Table 3-4, however, are not particularly supportive of the knowledgeability explanation outlined by Stipak. Street conditions, for example, are surely as specific, tangible, and immediate as rat sightings and junk piles, yet the association between subjective problem and objective condition is very weak for street conditions.

Perhaps a more useful approach for understanding the general problem of discrepancy between citizens' perceptions and objective conditions is the "positive bias" argument. Stipak (1980: 10) marshals an impressive range of research findings showing that, in a broad variety of domains, people's reports of the quality of their living conditions have a positive bias:

> Campbell *et al.* (1976, p. 99) found high levels of expressed satisfaction for a variety of different life domains. Only a small minority of the respondents admitted dissatisfaction or unhappiness . . . [this] agrees with the general finding from psychological research that subjects tend to use the positive side of rating

The Neighborhood Context

TABLE 3-4. *Associations Between Specific Measures of Objective Conditions and Residents' Perceptions of Those Problems*

Survey Item*	Objective Conditions Indicator	Gamma Coefficient
Mosquitoes, rats, or similar pests	Reported rat sightings per 1,000 dwelling units	.406
Trash piles, junk, or weeds on people's property	Number of random sites at which trained observers found trash piles or junk objects	.349
Weeds or high grass	Number of random sites at which trained observers found weeds or grass over 1 foot high	.355
Potholes or streets in bad repair	Average rating by trained observers of street conditions across the random sites	.185
Flooding when it storms	Cost per thousand dwelling units to correct all storm sewer drainage problems	.058
Composite perceived need measure	Composite objective and measure	.292

*The items were presented as follows: Now I will read a list of possible problems. Could you tell me whether each one is a big problem, somewhat of a problem, or not a problem at all in your neighborhood.

scales more than the negative side.... [There is also] evidence ... that people tend to evaluate more favorably their own lives and experiences, including experiences with government agencies, than the lives and experiences of other people.

A closer look at the Kansas City data suggests that positive bias is indeed at work. Specifically, Table 3-1, which details the relationship between objective need and perceived need should be reconsidered. Some respondents from objectively "better-off" neighborhoods point to a surprising number of problems in their neighborhood, but the reverse pattern is much more common. More than one-third of the respondents from the objectively "worst-off" neighborhoods identified no big problems in their neighborhood, and a little more than half identified either one or no big problems.

Research on the general discrepancy between objective and subjective measures, and particularly the "positive bias" explanation for this slippage, thus helps to clarify why the link between objective and perceived need is no stronger than it is. Problems must be perceived before they are politicized; and the positive bias argument suggests that there are social-psychological dynamics that inhibit acknowledgment of problems.

Perhaps the most surprising finding from the foregoing analysis, however, is that perceived inequality is the strongest of the predictors of perceived need—considerably stronger than objective conditions in the neighborhood. The positive bias argument, outlined above, suggests that citizens are inclined to believe that their circumstances are as good as anyone else's, if not better. This conception inhibits their ability to recognize problems. Presumably, however, when confronted with evidence (or rumor) that other neighborhoods *are* "better-off," this positive bias wears thin. Conditions that might not have seemed problematic become so when it is believed that residents of other neighborhoods do not have to put up with them.

The data at hand do not allow for an assessment of the reasons why citizens conclude that conditions are better in other neighborhoods or which neighborhoods they have used for comparison. If anything, the weak association between perceived inequality and objective need ($r = .16$) suggests that residents of neighborhoods at many different levels of quality find reason to believe that other neighborhoods are still better off. Furthermore, it may be that processes other than delivery of urban services yield the apparent differences in quality of life to which citizens react.

The important point, however, is that objective conditions in and of themselves are not direct predictors of demand-making. Objective conditions are important only insofar as they contribute to perceived need for government attention; and even in this regard, objective conditions in the neighborhood are not of primary importance. This is because perceived need is a form of problem definition—a process that has been found to be more heavily influenced by expectations than by objective conditions facing the resident. In particular, when citizens' expectations are heightened because they believe other neighborhoods are better served, we find higher levels of perceived need and fertile ground for demand-making.

Neighborhood Organization as a Contextual Factor in Demand-Making

An earlier chapter explored the need-awareness model developed by Jones and colleagues (1977) to explain differential volumes of complaints from different Detroit neighborhoods. That model was found to be wanting when applied to individual contacting behavior. Need (at least perceived need) is an important predictor of contacting behavior, but awareness (knowledge of government officials) is not; and the hypothesized interaction effect of need and awareness does not appear when we examine contacting propensity across levels of socioeconomic status.

Here, however, the need-awareness model must be temporarily resurrected. Its failure to account for individual behavior in Kansas City does not necessarily mean that it is not useful for predicting contacting propensity across neighborhoods. Perhaps more important, the model provides a useful framework within which to pursue the theme that, apart from individual characteristics, the social context in which the individual is located may have important effects.

More specifically, we are interested in the possibility that, if the need-awareness model is not a totally satisfactory explanation of variation in contacting across neighborhoods, it is because some neighborhoods, with certain neighborhood organization characteristics, alter the pattern of contacting from what the need-awareness model predicts. Stated another way, the predictive power of the need-awareness model may be limited because it omits a crucial explanatory factor—neighborhood organization activity.

That neighborhood organizations have proliferated and play a "parapolitical" role is by now a commonplace observation in the study of urban politics (Lipsky and Levi, 1972; Bell and Held, 1969; O'Brien, 1975). In particular, it is frequently argued that neighborhood organizations contribute to the demands being made upon urban government. Yates argues: "If policemen, firemen, and teachers are the foot soldiers of city governments, then members of these neighborhood groups are the foot soldiers of the community in dealing with city government. They take the lead in pressing complaints and in fighting city hall. They are the principal neighborhood combatants in the many-sided contest of urban politics" (1977: 25).

Curiously, however, this prevailing wisdom about the role of neighborhood organizations in generating demands has not been substantiated in research on the antecedents of citizen-initiated contacting. Rather, this form of demand-making has been viewed as a purely individualistic act of political assertion—a view perhaps attributable to Verba and Nie's (1972) conclusions that contacting is the peculiar preserve of a group of "parochial participants" who are, by and large, uninvolved with group problem-solving or other forms of political activity, and whose "interests in government activity appear to be limited to the ways that activity affects their personal lives." Consequently, research on citizen-initiated contacting has focused primarily on either individual attributes or need-related neighborhood conditions. The one exception, Jones's (1981) Chicago-based analysis, found no evidence that community organizations have a stimulative effect on demand-making, but instead that party organizations do.

There are, however, sound reasons for hypothesizing that neighborhood organizations may affect the propensity of individuals to register demands with urban officials. As Eisinger (1972) notes, the prospect of approaching city hall may intimidate many citizens who are unfamiliar with the workings of local government. Neighborhood organizations might play a crucial mediating role here, providing residents with information about whom to contact, encouraging such demand-making to secure benefits for the neighborhood, and perhaps even actively forwarding complaints on behalf of neighborhood residents. Although no existing research specifically documents this role, Sharp (1980a) has found that, particularly for the poor, less-educated, and minority citizens, neighborhood organizations are recognized as important alternatives to direct confrontations with government officials.

As noted in the preceding section, however, the effect of neighborhood organizations on contacting propensity is surely contingent on the organization's characteristics. Some neighborhoods have low-key, inactive homeowners' associations. Even active, well-organized groups differ in the extent to which they view a "parapolitical" role as appropriate. The leaders of some organizations may encourage demand-making; others may be preoccupied with other matters or not interested in facilitating citizens' contacts with government officials.

To the extent that the impact of neighborhood organizations is contingent on these multiple and relatively subtle features of the organization, comparative case analysis, based on more in-depth information about neighborhood organizations, is needed. Interviews with the leaders of neighborhood organizations serving each of the study neighborhoods provided the information for such a comparative case analysis.[4]

To determine the impact of neighborhood organizations, however, a mechanism is needed for isolating "unusual" neighborhoods, those where the level of citizen-initiated contacting is substantially higher or lower than might be expected. Jones and colleagues' (1977) need-awareness model provides the crucial framework here, for it specifies the types of neighborhoods that should have the highest and lowest contacting propensity.

The need-awareness model posits that contacting propensity should be high only where there are sufficient levels both of need for government services and of awareness of government. Where either factor is at a low level (and presumably, especially where both are low) we should expect to find fewer citizen contacts with government.

The twenty-four Kansas City study neighborhoods can be arrayed against these two criteria, using neighborhood-level versions of the measures of perceived need and knowledge of government officials (i.e., awareness). Figure 3-4 shows such a plotting of the study neighborhoods, by average perceived need and the mean number of government entities that respondents for the neighborhood were able to identify. The grid is divided into quadrants at the overall means of the two variables.

In Chapter 2 it was pointed out that one of the difficulties of the need-awareness model is that it presumes knowledge of the threshold levels of need and awareness. Here, the overall means for perceived need and awareness are used as rough approximations of such thresholds. Neighborhoods in Quadrant I are higher than average on both need and awareness. These areas should be especially prone to contacting. Neighborhoods in Quadrants II and IV are above average on one factor but below average on the other, and neighborhoods in Quadrant III are below average on both. All these neighborhoods, and especially those in Quadrant III, should show relatively low levels of contacting.

Figure 3-4 also shows two measures of contacting propensity in each neighborhood (in parentheses below the neighborhood name). On the left is the percentage of respondents who said they had contacted an official; on the right is a volume-oriented measure of contacting propensity. Respondents who said they had contacted an official were asked how many such contacts they made in the last year. The right-hand number in each parentheses is the total number of contacts reported divided by the appropriate survey N for the neighborhood, or total contacts per survey respondent.[5]

Table 3-5 provides a summary of the power of the need-

The Neighborhood Context 85

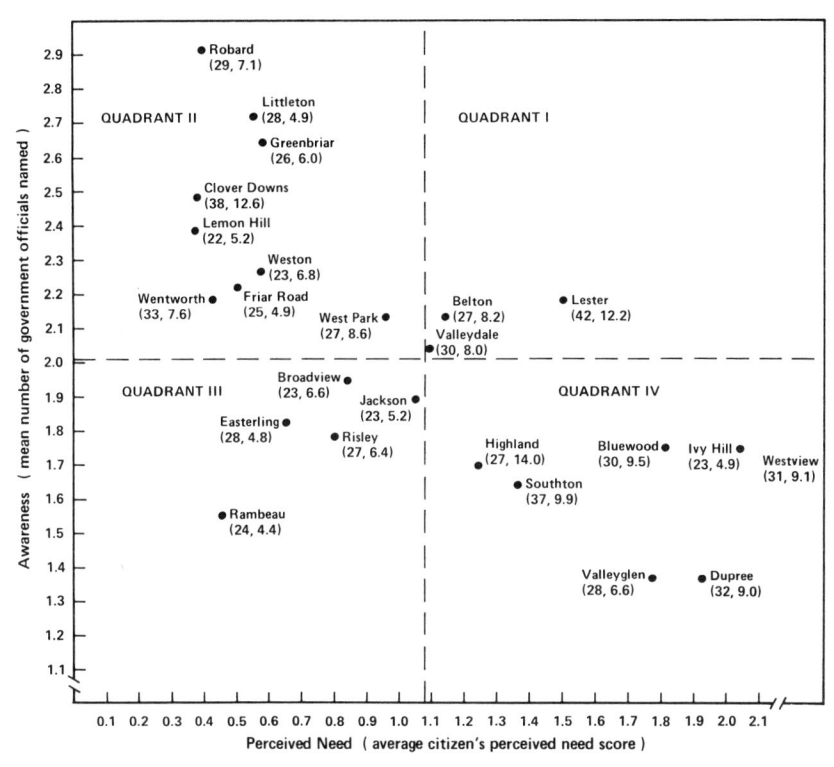

FIGURE 3-4. *Need, Awareness, and Contacting Propensity: 24 Kansas City Study Neighborhoods*

awareness model in accounting for neighborhood-level variation in contacting propensity. Respondents from Quadrant I neighborhoods, where both need and awareness are above average, are the most prone to have made a contact and have made the highest number of contacts, just as the need-awareness model would predict. Differences in contacting propensity across the four quadrants are small, however, especially with respect to the percentage of citizens who have made a contact.

Figure 3-4, shows that these differences are small because some of the neighborhoods show contacting propensities consistent with the need-awareness model but some do not. In Quadrant

TABLE 3-5. *Need-Awareness Status of the Neighborhood and Contacting Propensity*

Quadrant	Type of Neighborhood	Percent Who Have Contacted	(N)	Contacts per Respondent
I	High need-high awareness	33	(271)	9.5
II	Low need-high awareness	28	(794)	7.1
III	Low need-low awareness	25	(455)	5.5
IV	High need-low awareness	30	(628)	9.0
	Total	28	(2148)	7.6

$Chi^2 = 6.20$ Eta $= .55$
Sig. $= .10$
Cramer's V $= .05$

I, for example, the Lester neighborhood exhibits a high level of contacting propensity, as the model would predict; but the Belton and Valleydale neighborhoods show only average levels of contacting propensity. Low levels of contacting would be expected in Quadrant II neighborhoods. This is true of neighborhoods such as Lemon Hill and Weston but not of Clover Downs. In Quadrant IV also, conditions are not favorable for demand-making, according to the need-awareness model. Although the below-average level of contacting in Ivy Hill is consistent with these expectations, other neighborhoods, particularly Southton, show surprisingly high levels of contacting.

In short, the need-awareness model allows us to isolate exceptional neighborhoods—those where contacting is either higher or lower than expected. An exceptional neighborhood is one with some context that has an impact on contacting propensity beyond what the need and awareness factors would suggest. The hypothesis here is that neighborhood organization activity may be a key to understanding these neighborhoods. In the comparative case analysis that follows, information from interviews with neighborhood organization leaders is introduced as evidence for this hypothesis.

Neighborhood Associations and Contacting: A Comparative Case Analysis

Quadrant I, Figure 3-4 contains three neighborhoods. One of these—Lester—exhibits the high level of contacting that the need-awareness model predicts for neighborhoods with its characteristics. In the other two neighborhoods—Valleydale and Belton—contacting propensity is about average. The following comparative case analysis provides some clues to neighborhood organization dynamics that may help to account for these differences.

Lester is a predominantly white neighborhood of low or moderate income people. Its neighborhood association is five years old. When asked what he would do if a resident came to the association with a problem involving city service, the president said, "You can always call the Action Center, of course." He went on to explain that the Action Center "really is a good method for a lot of people to use" because most "aren't skilled in working through the process." The Action Center is "skilled in listening" to a problem and referring the caller to the right place. He noted, however, "I call direct myself"—that is, when he has a complaint or request to make, he calls a department head or other official directly because it is faster than going through the Action Center referral process. But everyone who calls him for advice on city service problems is told, "You gotta start through the process." When asked if the association ever makes complaints on behalf of individuals, he said that sometimes it does but that "people gotta learn how to help themselves."

The organization is clearly developing connections to city government apart from the Action Center. City council members and the local state representative come to meetings and, "quite often" someone from the city bureaucracy also attends. The respondent emphasized that the organization has moved from quiescence to aggressiveness. In the past, he said, "we have not gotten our share" but "we're a lot better now—more insistent." When asked how the group is insistent, he explained that, if necessary, councilman Valequez[6] could be approached because he is very responsive, and Councilman DiCarlo is "from the Northeast" (a reference to the larger area of which the neighborhood is a part). The respondent emphasized that citizens should try to be reasonable, but they must be persistent in dealing with the city.

As we will see in the following chapter, this neighborhood is not particularly high on contacts to the Action Center—the city's centralized complaint-handling unit. This neighborhood leader's ambivalence about the Action Center (it is important for those who do not know their way through city hall, but there are better, more direct methods) is consistent with that finding. But the neighborhood is very high on citizen contacts with local officials generally (see Figure 3-4), and the neighborhood organization leader's comments suggest some possible reasons for this high level.

Compared with some of the others that will be examined, the organization is relatively well-organized and active and therefore presumably fairly visible in the community. The leader actively encourages demand-making, emphasizing to residents that "you gotta start through the process" and that the neighborhood gets its fair share of benefits only when people are insistent. In addition, the organization provides access to a variety of city officials—some are invited to meetings—and the leader knows which council members are approachable.

This situation can be contrasted with that in the Belton neighborhood, which is served by the Wilmington-Wabash Improvement Association.

> The Wilmington-Wabash organization has been in existence, at least in its current form, for two years. The respondent, chairman of the board of directors, explained that the group was reorganized recently. It has been having difficulty replacing older members as they left the board.
> The organization is working on an "energy audit" and weatherization program. It has done some small-scale housing rehabilitation. It had a tool bank so tools could be loaned for repair projects until a series of thefts of the tools put a damper on

this project. The only other current project is a community garden, cosponsored by several area colleges.

Most of the organization's plans remain unimplemented. One goal is to help people get home repair loans, but no way has been found to do so. It would also like to get authorization to do a weatherization project on a vacant school building and convert it for use as a community building. Finally, it wants to have the city council "designate the area as one for federal help," but this effort has not gotten very far.

When asked what would happen if a resident came to the organization with a problem or request about city services, the chairman explained that the organization would contact the city council representative first, then the mayor, to "see if we can't find out who and where to get help." He was not aware of the Action Center as a possibility; when asked about it, he confused it with a community action center "somewhere down on Main Street." Furthermore, he was not sanguine about the results the organization has achieved when it has made demands upon city government. As an example, he cited problems with people dumping trash in the neighborhood. "By going through all the red tape" (contacting city officials), the organization can sometimes get the trash removed, but not always. So it has resorted to more direct methods such as poring through the mail in trash piles to discover who the trash belonged to.

The respondent indicated that the neighborhood has been "overlooked for some time" by the city and is still struggling to get the attention and help it deserves. "They [city officials] know we are here now," but so far city officials have shown no willingness to help with the neighborhood's problems.

If neighborhood organizations can be crucial catalysts that mobilize residents for high levels of demand-making, the Wilmington-Wabash association exemplifies one that is unlikely to play such a role. It seems to lack strong organization and leadership and appears to be in a holding pattern between the failures of previously attempted activities and the as-yet-to-be-implemented endeavors that are on its agenda. The organization's spokesperson had only a vague notion of what might be done to assist residents with urban service problems—the inclination is to assume that, as problems arise, elected officials can be asked for advice on whom to go to for help. Rather than viewing complaints and service requests as critical forms of demand-making that will generate important benefits for the neighborhood, this respondent thinks of the red tape this process involves. Finally, the organization appears to be waiting for city officials to demonstrate commitment to the neighborhood rather than insistently pressing for a variety of specific responses.

The Valleydale neighborhood in Quadrant I of Figure 3-4, like Belton, shows only an average level of contacting propensity even though need and awareness levels are relatively high. Unlike Belton's neighborhood association, however, the Valleydale Neighborhood Association appears to be well-organized and active. Other considerations, however, militate against its encouragement of certain forms of demand-making.

> The Valleydale organization was formed in 1976 at the time of a protest over the closing of a fire station. Since then, it has pursued a variety of activities, including crime prevention programs, a neighborhood conservation effort in conjunction with the city's systematic codes enforcement program, and working with the Action Center on "spot problems."
>
> The organization takes a very active role in channeling problems regarding city services to the Action Center. The president encourages people to do this and explains that most people do not know how the Action Center works. She explains that it is a "pipeline" to the relevant department and that the Action Center "keeps you apprised and asks you to grade the response." She keeps a three-year backlog of Action Center reports, "so we can tell where things are."
>
> The organization also works directly with some city departments and makes major efforts to inform citizens about city agencies. It frequently has guest speakers for its meetings to expose members to government officials. She explained that "it is very important that people be educated on how the departments work." In addition, each spring she encourages citizens to submit

The Neighborhood Context

a list of streets with potholes. When this approach was first tried, two Street Department people came out and toured the streets in question. She claimed that "because of our interest and acting with them as inspectors, we received quite a bit more work than was scheduled." The major agenda for the organization now, she said, is "maintenance"—the streets need to be kept a little cleaner, a few housing maintenance problems need to be attended to, and new curbs, gutters, and sidewalks are needed. But she explained that she would not push the latter issue because much of the neighborhood population is elderly, and she wants to avoid any projects that might cause higher taxes or special assessments. Similarly, her organization is "not into re-habbing houses" as many neighborhood groups are. She explained that many of the residents are elderly homeowners, and the housing stock is "basically pretty good." Hence she does not believe a major housing rehabilitation effort is appropriate.

The Valleydale Neighborhood Association clearly encourages demand-making with respect to the basic housekeeping services of city government. The Action Center is viewed as a key resource, and the Street Department is another avenue for presenting aggregated neighborhood demands. The volume of contacts with the Action Center emanating from this neighborhood is indeed very high. When all types of contacts with city government are considered as in Figure 3-4, however, this neighborhood does not appear to be very contact prone, despite its high need and awareness levels and despite the existence of an apparently active, visible, and well-organized neighborhood association.

A close reading of the respondent's comments suggests that the organization encourages demand-making directed in specific channels but neglects other potential demands because of sensitivity to the characteristics of the local population. The organization has developed specific ways to encourage reporting of street repair and code enforcement problems. Demands for broader housing redevelopment efforts are not to be encouraged, however, because elderly citizens in their small but "adequate" frame houses are an important constituency for this organization. Similarly, curbs, gutters, and sidewalks are needed, but demands for them might mean special assessments that the elderly residents would not want to bear, so these demands are not encouraged.

In short, this organization might usefully be viewed as a "special-purpose" catalyst for demand-making, in contrast with the general-purpose demand encouragement that the Lester organization pursues. It encourages limited demand-making, but it acts to constrain a variety of potential demands. Hence the overall level of citizen-initiated complaints and service requests from this neighborhood is not maximized.

Neighborhoods in Quadrant II of Figure 3-4 differ in an important respect from those in Quadrant I: awareness of government is high, but perceived need is not. In fact, Quadrant II incorporates all of the study neighborhoods that would be recognized locally as the best-off neighborhoods in Kansas City. Hence, according to the need-awareness model, high levels of citizen-initiated contacting in these neighborhoods would not be expected.

One neighborhood, however—Clover Downs—has an exceptionally high level of contacting, in terms of both the percentage of respondents who have contacted an official and the volume of contacts per survey respondent. Clover Downs generated more survey-reported contacts per respondent than the Lester neighborhood in Quadrant I.

> Clover Downs is one of a group of subdivisions on the city's southwest side that make up a planned development called the Country Club District. Within this district, each subdivision has a homes association, responsible among other things for enforcing deed restrictions that govern the use of property in this planned development. An umbrella organization, the Homes Associations of Country Club District (HACCD), provides bookkeeping, central office, and coordinating services for the individual homes associations. The central purpose of the homes associations approach is to preserve the character of all of the subdivisions in

The Neighborhood Context

the planned development. The carefully maintained, fine brick homes and immaculately manicured lawns and greenbelts in the area testify to the success of the concept.

The Clover Downs Homes Association, established in 1920, is a member of the HACCD. The group's major activities involve enforcement and reporting of building code violations, maintenance of the various "islands" (parkway greenbelts) that have statuary or stone walls needing periodic repair, contracting for their own snow removal service when winters are harsh and residents request it, a crime watch program, and a tree planting program.

When residents have problems with city services, the organization takes the matter to the umbrella organization, HACCD, which forwards it to the Action Center. The respondent for the Clover Downs association commented: "We use it [the Action Center] all the time; we don't hesitate to report problems whenever they are called to our attention. We have gotten very good response." Building code violations, on the other hand, are reported directly to the city building department.

The biggest problem in the neighborhood, according to this respondent, is the "maintenance of values." The main concern is the maintenance of property values in the neighborhood because "one rotten apple in the middle of the barrel makes the whole barrel go bad."

Although the respondent believed that city officials were generally very receptive to the organization, he also believed that neighborhoods like Clover Downs are less likely to get neighborhood improvement funds because "it is not politically popular to give money to the rich." The assumption is that they will not get "their fair share of money for renovation and general upkeep of the neighborhood."

This brief case description provides some important clues to the unexpectedly high level of citizen-initiated contacting in Clover Downs. The homes association encourages the activity, and referral of complaints and service requests through the umbrella HACCD may be perceived as adding more clout. But this is surely not the whole story, for the level of perceived need in the neighborhood is low; consequently, even this form of facilitation would not normally be expected to generate an extraordinary volume of citizen requests and complaints.

Perceived need, however, has to do with the extent to which residents identify "big problems" in their neighborhoods. Perhaps subtle forms of perceived need are prevalent in Clover Downs, as indicated by the pair of interrelated themes articulated by the Clover Downs Homes Association respondent—the "one rotten apple" theme and a "system bias" theme. The respondent believes that this neighborhood's greatest interest is the protection of property values, which can be threatened by even one "rotten apple." Such a perspective suggests the importance of monitoring and reporting incipient problems before they become "big problems." It is for this reason that the organization stresses active reporting of building code violations.

There is also a presumption that the character of city politics will militate against allocation of "renovation and general upkeep" resources to the neighborhood. City officials may be responsive in delivering basic services, but the "extras" are presumed to be slated for poor neighborhoods.

To the extent that these perspectives are broadly shared in the neighborhood, citizen-initiated contacts take on added importance. If the neighborhood is unlikely to get special attention in any macropolicy decision making, then individualistic demands, geared toward nipping any potential problems in the bud, become an important method for pursuing the goal of "maintenance of values." In short, the Clover Downs case illustrates the possibility that, even in a neighborhood where residents do not experience "big problems," a neighborhood association might help to establish a sense that there are special needs; and if city officials do not view the neighborhood as needing special attention, particularized demand-making focused on nascent problems is a key strategy.

Finally, let us consider the neighborhoods in Quadrant IV of Figure 3-4. These are ones that the need-awareness model would predict to be low on contacting because, although need is high, awareness is not. Again, we find exceptions—most notably the Southton neighborhood, where the proportion of residents who have contacted an official is unusually high, and Highland, where the number of survey-reported contacts per respondent is unusually high. An examination of the characteristics of neighborhood organizations in these areas, particularly in comparison with those of an organization in a neighborhood such as Ivy Hill (where contacting propensity is low, as expected), should be revealing.

The Southton Neighborhood Association has between three and four hundred members, and its president has an active agenda to encourage gentrification. The association is pushing on a variety of fronts to remove any obstacles to attracting young professionals to fix up homes and move into the neighborhood.

Specifically, the organization is pressuring the city for code enforcement, is involved in the city's paint-up program, and is working to get areas on two major boulevards declared historic districts. It also has active block watch and home security programs. Finally, it has pressed the Liquor Control Board to do something about the concentration of liquor establishments and has debated with HUD officials about Section 8 housing problems in the area.

The president claimed that, over the years, he has referred all problems that members have asked him about to the city. He went on to explain that, in past years, people, especially the elderly, hesitated to call the Action Center because they would have to give their names. Now the complaints are made for them by the association, and the mail regarding the problem comes to him. He commented that people have found "through a decade of experience" that, if one goes directly to a department, the request dies; but because the Action Center requires a report from the department and sends an evaluation card, working with it brings results.

More generally, the respondent believes that the neighborhood has some clout. He argued that when an individual needs something, especially one of the "larger things that cost money," he or she gets no response. But the organization "represents 1,700 votes" and can get the city council to consider such things.

The respondent emphasized the importance of making demands. From his perspective, it takes repeated and prolonged pushing to get what you want from the city because the "squeaky wheel gets the oil." Furthermore, it is not enough for an individual citizen to get his or her problem settled. People, he said, tend to come to a meeting when they have a problem, and when it is resolved, they go away. It took "a lot of indoctrination" to get residents to understand that "a problem six blocks away is also theirs."

With this background information about the neighborhood organization, Southton's high level of citizen-initiated contacts with government officials is considerably less surprising. The organization clearly encourages such demand-making by publicizing the advantages of the Action Center, forwarding complaints for elderly citizens who are unwilling to press matters on their own, and persuading residents to take a collective, neighborhood view of potential service delivery problems. These characteristics, coupled with the organization's active agenda and high visibility, suggest that the organization may be responsible for raising the level of demand-making above that predicted by the need-awareness model.

The Highland neighborhood also shows an exceptional level of contacting propensity. The comments of its neighborhood organization leaders (both the current president and a board member were interviewed) suggest that the reasons for this involvement may be more subtle than the straightforward, neighborhood organization promotion of demand-making found in the Southton neighborhood.

> The Highland neighborhood is the locus for considerable gentrification — many upwardly mobile, young professionals have moved in to reclaim some of the old, historic mansions for residences. Many of these people are lawyers, and the Highland Neighborhood Council leaders interviewed acknowledged that they tend to dominate in the neighborhood council.
> The organization has a broad variety of programs, the most active of which is an "ongoing zoning watchdog program." The

president explained that many lawyers live in the neighborhood and that they are always fighting to keep property uses in line with zoning restrictions.

Both respondents believed that the organization had good access to city officials and carried political weight. According to the president, the neighborhood is special because it constitutes a pocket of young professionals who are energetic and politically active. He claimed that voter turnout is high and that elected officials pay close attention to the neighborhood. The other respondent claimed that the residents "know a lot of people on the zoning board and other things" and that city officials "know that if we need to we can get a bunch of people to go down there."

With respect to citizen demands and complaints, the respondent explained that "there are certain people that specialize in things like that—a lot of lawyers in the neighborhood." Such individuals give advice on what to do. The association's president noted that he gets a couple of phone calls a week from residents with problems, many of which involve code violations. There are two ways to handle these, he said. They "have had a very good response from the Action Center . . . it seems to follow up on every single complaint." But he sees referring residents to the Action Center as "the passive way" of dealing with problems. Neighborhood association leaders have taken more active roles, ranging from writing letters to relevant units with copies to council members, to bringing nuisance actions. In fact, he acknowledged that the association is "very quick to resort to legal action."

He sees the neighborhood's high rate of demand-making as understandable—"it is most easily explained by the new population in the neighborhood." Those who moved in are "urban pioneers," who owe their success to their own energies and who moved in expecting to invest energy in the neighborhood and to fight to make it what they want it to be.

The Highland neighborhood's higher-than-expected contacting propensity is not, apparently, purely a result of encouragement and facilitation by the neighborhood organization. Rather, both its level of demand-making and the characteristics of its neighborhood association reflect an unusually active, albeit minority population—the gentrifying element of the area. Many of these individuals have professional skills and orientations that make complaint-filing a matter-of-course activity rather than an unusual act requiring the mediating efforts of a community group. The neighborhood association has served as an organizing locus for these individuals. Residents are not dependent upon a neighborhood organization for advice on demand-making, however; if anything, the reverse is true.

In somewhat different ways, then, the neighborhood associations in Southton and Highland help to account for the unexpectedly high levels of demand-making in these two areas. Both cases can be contrasted with the Ivy Hill neighborhood association.

The Ivy Hill Neighborhood Council is a small, informal neighborhood association. The respondent for this association emphasized that none of its activities have received external, financial support and that when "white flight" hit the neighborhood, it lost its political strength.

The organization's leaders have distinctly adversarial relationships with city government, which the respondent described as "stand-off enemies." He claimed that when the whites moved out, the city marked the area for a new freeway and apparently hoped the neighborhood would deteriorate so the property could be condemned. The association asked for money to help residents deal with housing problems but was turned down. A city initiative for cooperative provision of street-salting and weed-cutting services broke down because the Ivy Hill leadership thought there were too many strings attached, and the city would not provide compensation for injuries that might occur.

Despite these strained relationships with the city, the neighborhood association does refer problems to the Action Center. The respondent said that he was very familiar with the Action Center and had found it to do a good job most of the time. When asked if the association ever contacts anyone else in city government with problems, he indicated that it did not. When the Action Center cannot solve a problem, the neighborhood organization "has learned to take care of our own."

Unlike Southton and Highland, the Ivy Hill neighborhood does not exhibit an exceptional level of demand-making; and, unlike Southton's and Highland's, Ivy Hill's neighborhood association shows no special features or circumstances that might facilitate demand-making. If anything, the strained relations between the neighborhood and city hall inhibit demand-making; from this neighborhood leader's perspective, the Action Center is the only usable problem-solving channel.

Neighborhood organizations thus can make a difference in mobilizing residents for demand-making. As the foregoing comparative case analysis shows, however, there are a variety of different ways in which organizations do this, and there are many organizations that fail to do so. Some neighborhood organizations truly are the "foot soldiers" in the "street fighting pluralism" of which Yates (1977) speaks. Others, for a variety of reasons, act less effectively as mobilizing agents for demand-making. In sum, neighborhood organization activity is variable, but it may be at least as important as need and awareness in accounting for the differential levels of demand-making across urban neighborhoods.

Summary

This chapter has considered a variety of aspects of the neighborhood context that may have a bearing on the demand-making process. In differing ways, attention to various aspects of the neighborhood context helps to enrich understanding of contacting propensity.

For example, the relevance of the socioeconomic model is in part contingent on the socioeconomic character of the neighborhood. In neighborhoods with high levels of average educational attainment, there are striking differences in contacting propensity by education level—differences that are not so evident in neighborhoods of lower average educational attainment.

Objective conditions are part of the neighborhood context as well. Differences in these constitute important differences in objective need for government attention. Objective need is not, however, a direct predictor of demand-making. It is modestly associated with perceived need, however, and the latter is a key predictor of demand-making. But there is far from a one-on-one correspondence between objective and perceived need. A "positive bias" in individuals' perceptions of their living conditions is one reason for this lack of correspondence. In addition, differences in citizens' expectations can create differing levels of perceived need, objective conditions being equal. In particular, beliefs that other neighborhoods are better served are more powerful than objective conditions themselves in generating perceptions of need.

A more in-depth analysis of differences in the characteristics of neighborhood organizations suggests a variety of ways in which such organizations may serve to facilitate demand-making. Some neighborhoods exhibit levels of citizen-initiated contacting that are reasonably in accord with what the need-awareness model would predict; others exhibit unexpectedly high levels of contacting. Among the latter, we find that neighborhood organizations are active in a variety of ways to facilitate demand-making. Some act in a mediating role, referring problems to appropriate channels; others demonstrate the importance of demand-making for the good of the neighborhood; still others provide a focal point for the aggressive, demand-making instincts of a set of gentrifying professionals.

In Chapter 1, a variety of limitations of the socioeconomic and the need-awareness models were discussed. Here we see that, in addition to these limitations, both explanations are limited in yet another way. Each is elegantly simple but provides only a skeletal framework for understanding the demand-making process. Analysis of the richly varied contexts of urban neighborhood life suggests important dynamics that are not included in either of the basic explanatory models of citizen-initiated contacting.

The Neighborhood Context

NOTES TO CHAPTER 3

1. Here, as in all other chapters, pseudonyms rather than actual neighborhood names are used to ensure the anonymity of neighborhood organization leaders who were interviewed.

2. With the exception of the housing value measure, all measures are such that higher values indicate more extensive problems (i.e., greater objective need). To mesh the housing value measure with the others, the signs of the standardized housing value scores were reversed, that is, a greater than average housing value was treated as an equivalently lower than average level of objective housing need.

3. Although there is not, strictly speaking, interval-level measurement here, all variables are either dichotomous or involve strong ordinal measurement. Hence correlational methods of analysis are used.

4. In three of the neighborhoods, no functioning neighborhood organization could be located, and in one, contact with the leadership of the neighborhood organization could not be established. For most neighborhoods, the City Development Department's mapping of extant neighborhood associations, coupled with information from either city staff or informants from umbrella community organizations provided a clear indication of the relevant neighborhood association for the study neighborhood and frequently a contact person as well. Open-ended interviews were conducted, by telephone, with the leaders of each of these organizations—usually the president or chair of the board of directors. The interview protocol consisted of a small set of questions asking the respondent to describe the organization's activities, its relationship with city government, most important problems facing the neighborhood, and usual tactics when citizens ask for advice on problems involving delivery of city services.

5. Total survey-reported rather than agency-reported contacts are used because the only agency-recorded contacting data available are from the Action Center. As Chapter 4 shows, contacts to the Action Center represent a minority of all contacts—most contacts are made directly to the relevant city operating department. Comparable, geo-codable data from even the major operating departments were not available for this study.

6. As with neighborhoods, pseudonyms are used for all persons mentioned.

4
What Difference Does a Central Complaints Unit Make?

☑ ☑ ☐
☑ ☑ ☐

So far, contacts have been treated as all of a kind, irrespective of the target. It is necessary to consider whether contacts to a centralized complaint-handling unit are subsuming other avenues of contact, whether the existence of such a unit has an impact on patterns of contacting, and whether there is evidence that government is more responsive to contacts lodged with that unit. Each of these possibilities constitutes a potential impact that a centralized complaint-handling unit such as Kansas City's Action Center might be expected to have.

In one respect, the Action Center could be said to have very little impact because it clearly has not supplanted other avenues of access to city hall for complaints and requests. Even though it is relatively well-known,[1] the Action Center is apparently not the predominant channel for such contacts in Kansas City. Instead, as Table 4-1 shows, survey respondents reported that most of their contacts are made directly to the specific city departments responsible for delivery of services. The next most common (though far less so) avenue is one that might be expected of a citizen who has no clear idea of an appropriate channel of access for a specific problem—simply calling city hall. The relatively small percentage of citizens using this approach is roughly matched by the percentage who said that they make their request or complaint through the Action Center. Finally, there were scattered mentions of a variety of other contact targets, ranging from the mayor to a city council member to a neighborhood leader to the city attorney, the public information office, or the city man-

TABLE 4-1. *Targets of Citizen-Initiated Contacts*

Point of Contact	Percent
Specific city department	52
City hall	15
Action Center	14
Other	19
	100
(N)	(525)

ager's office. No single one of these was mentioned by more than 3 percent of the contactors.

If the Action Center is not the predominant access channel, however, we might expect that certain subgroups of the population would be more dependent on it than others. Centralized complaint-handling units, for example, could be viewed as particularly important to the urban "underclass" (Lineberry, 1977), who have fewer connections with the city bureaucracy.

Tables 4-2 and 4-3, however, present contrary patterns. Table 4-2 indicates that the importance of the Action Center as a contacting channel is virtually invariant across the four education groups. Channels for contacting do differ across education groups, but the difference is primarily a trade-off between approaching a specific city department and relying upon a nondirective call to city hall. The former avenue is increasingly likely across the education categories, and the latter is inversely associated with education. In short, there is no evidence that the Action Center is especially heavily used by the less-educated.

Table 4-3 is even more damaging to the notion that a centralized complaints unit might be an especially important mediator for minority citizens in dealing with bureaucracy. If anything, the table shows that white citizens are heavier users of the Action Center than are black or other minority ethnic groups.

Table 4-3 is especially surprising because the Action Center has a black director. Thomas (1982) found, in his Cincinnati

TABLE 4-2. *Targets of Citizen-Initiated Contacts, by Education (percentages)*

Target of Contact	Years of Education			
	1–11	12	13–16	17–21
Specific city department	42	52	54	60
City hall	27	16	13	5
Action Center	12	17	13	13
Other	19	15	20	22
	100	100	100	100
(N)	(95)	(149)	(221)	(60)

Chi^2 = 19.87 Sig. = .02
Cramer's V = .11

TABLE 4-3. *Targets of Citizen-Initiated Contacts, by Race (percentages)*

Target of Contact	Whites	Blacks	Other
Specific city department	53	50	52
City hall	12	26	31
Action Center*	16	7	3
Other	20	17	14
	101	100	100
(N)	(403)	(94)	(29)

*For proportions using the Action Center, two-tailed difference of proportions tests (between whites and blacks and whites and others) are significant at < .05 level.

study, that blacks were much more likely to call the Buildings and Inspections Department than whites and argued that this was because the department had a black department head. The presence of this official, he believes, "might have produced (1) a higher sense of efficacy among blacks who dealt with the department, (2) less systemic bias on the department's part in dealing with blacks, (3) a higher awareness of the department among blacks or (4) all three" (1982: 517–18). No such manifestation of "clientelism" based on racial identification emerges from the

Kansas City data, however, even though the Action Center, because of its black directorship, is as unusual in Kansas City as the Buildings and Inspections Department is in Cincinnati. None of the other major department heads in Kansas City who were interviewed for background information for this study were black.

This is not, of course, to say that the Action Center is not responsive to the problems of minority citizens. No evidence of such a bias was encountered. But the lack of use of the Action Center as an avenue of access by black and minority contactors (in Kansas City, the latter are predominantly Hispanic) deserved further exploration.

One reason why black and Hispanic respondents use the Action Center proportionately less than whites is that the former are less likely to know about the Action Center. More than two-fifths (42 percent) of white respondents correctly identified the Action Center; 37 percent of the blacks did so; and less than one-third (31 percent) of the Hispanic respondents knew about the Action Center. Although these differences in awareness are not extreme, they surely contribute to the lower levels of usage by blacks and Hispanics.

The means by which citizens found out about the Action Center ranged from word of mouth (friends, neighbors, or neighborhood organizations), the mass media (spots about the Action Center on television, radio, or in the newspapers), city advertising (the city used bus posters and inserts in water bills to advertise the Action Center's services), to information gleaned directly from a local government official. White, black, and Hispanic respondents gave virtually identical responses when asked about their sources of information about the Action Center. Each group learned about the Action Center predominantly from the mass media. Two-thirds of the Hispanic respondents, 70 percent of the blacks, and 74 percent of the white respondents found out about the Action Center from mass media sources. Next in importance was word of mouth. About one-fifth of the respondents in each group who knew about the Action Center found out about it from friends, neighbors, or individuals in their local community organization. Very few respondents gained their information directly from government officials or from the city's own advertising methods.

The comments of neighborhood organization leaders suggest additional reasons for minority citizens' low levels of Action Center usage. For example, the leader of a community organization in the predominantly Hispanic neighborhood included in this study saw good reasons why the Action Center would be less relevant in his neighborhood. He explained that, in recent years, the neighborhood has "grown in sophistication" and "knows how to work the system better." The citizens have a city council representative who is sympathetic to their needs, and "lots of problems go directly to his office." Furthermore, in the past, many of the major improvements they have gotten have been through "community organizing and political channels." For example, $1,750,000 was spent for new sidewalks, and he claimed that this action resulted from community organizing and pressure on elected officials in city hall.

Furthermore, there are many service-providing agencies in the neighborhood (he mentioned several nonprofit, volunteer agencies) that handle problems for people directly. He contrasted his neighborhood with some other inner city areas, where he said community life was "decimated" by urban redevelopment. These areas, he argued, "can't identify as a neighborhood," and they are "more dependent on individual methods" of getting help, such as calling the Action Center. In short, this Hispanic community leader believed that his neighborhood had ways of making demands that are more effective in gaining large-scale improvements than individual complaints about isolated problems would be. The latter, in his view, is what the Action Center approach represents.

Although this perspective is not echoed in the comments of leaders in every minority neighborhood, it is not an idiosyncratic view. In the predominantly black Bluewood[2] neighborhood, for example, the neighborhood organization president emphasized that there is a strong linkage between the neighborhood and city hall. The Action Center is not a factor in this linkage. Rather, the group contacts the city council member in the district to propose which streets, curbs, and gutters are in most need of repair. They even go as far as to propose a budget for the year for street repair in the neighborhood. The group also works with election groups and other political groups to support the candidate who will understand the needs of the neighborhood and will work with the neighborhood toward a common goal. "You know, I'll scratch your back and you scratch mine." The group also invites different city staff members to speak at its monthly meetings, often to explain issues or problems to the citizens. The organization mainly asks the city for improvement of its park. When citizens have a problem with city services, the organization brings it before its advisory committee to use the "group involvement" approach to problems. It is this group that collectively decides whether and whom to approach at city hall. Usually the problem is brought directly to a council member or the mayor, but depending on the nature of the complaint, it may be referred to a city department head.

Taken together, these comments suggest that, at least for some portion of the minority community in Kansas City, the Action Center is a less relevant avenue for demand-making than others. The Action Center is an institutional manifestation of reform government. It is a sympathetic but neutral tool for enhancing city government's responsiveness, and it is directly accountable to the city manager's office rather than to elected officials. Furthermore, it is designed to handle individual problems with service delivery promptly and professionally, not to serve as an advocate for neighborhood-level allocative decisions. For leaders of the minority community who advocate a more "political" approach and the importance of influencing major policy decisions rather than individual administrative remedies, other channels for demand-making, such as ties to city council members, are likely to be more salient. To the extent that neighborhood leaders can influence patterns of contacting in the neighborhood (see Chapter 3), it should not be surprising that the perspectives outlined above translate into relatively weak minority group usage of the Action Center.

In sum, we find that, at the individual level, the Action Center does not appear to have had a major impact. It does not serve as the primary access channel to local government for citizens, nor is it an especially important access channel for disadvantaged citizens.

Neighborhood-Level Patterns of Contacting

There is, however, another respect in which a central complaints unit like the Action Center does have an impact. The neighborhood-level pattern of demand-making via the Action Center might differ from the pattern of demands made through other channels. Specifically, we might hypothesize that contacting the Action Center may be more purely a function of neighborhood need than is contacting through traditional channels (council members, the mayor, and the like). Vedlitz, Dyer, and Durand (1980), for example, found that in Dallas and Houston, there is a negative, linear association between neighborhood social well-being and contacting propensity, rather than the parabolic pattern found by Jones and colleagues (1977) in Detroit. In other words, contacting in Dallas and Houston seemed to be a function of need only, rather than a function of need and awareness. Vedlitz, Dyer, and Durand offer the following possible explanation: "A centralized contacting system, which Dallas and Houston have but Detroit lacks, *may* [my emphasis] reduce the effect of awareness to the point at which contacts are substantially a function only of the need for services. . . . In cities with centralized reporting agencies, awareness of where and how to contact may be more equally distributed across all social well-being categories" (1980: 65).

Vedlitz, Dyer, and Durand's interpretation emphasizes differences in patterns of contacting across cities. I have adopted a similar hypothesis, but for differences across types of contacts within a single city. As we have seen, that Kansas City has a central complaints unit does not mean the bulk of contacts are targeted there. Rather, Action Center contacting is overlaid upon an existing and still dominant mosaic of contacts with a variety of other local officials and agencies. Like Vedlitz, Dyer, and Durand's interpretation, my hypothesis is that the volume of Action Center contacts emanating from a neighborhood is more closely associated with the neighborhood's need than contacting generally is because awareness of the Action Center is more equally distributed than awareness of channels of access to government generally.

To test this proposition, it is necessary to supplement the survey data with archival data on Action Center contacts. The volume of Action Center contacts reported on the random sample citizen survey is relatively small—too small to allow for comparisons between contacting the Action Center and all other forms of contacting at the neighborhood level. To provide a more accurate assessment of the volume of Action Center contacts emanating from the various neighborhoods, data from the Action Center's archives were used. Samples of both closed cases (from August 1981 through August 1982) and cases open as of the first half of October 1982 were drawn, and contactors' addresses were geo-coded to study neighborhoods.[3] To control for the differing populations of the study neighborhoods, the weighted total number of contacts from each neighborhood was divided by neighborhood population.

To derive a comparable measure of non-Action Center contacting propensity for each neighborhood (one reflecting a volume of contacts rather than a proportion of citizens contacting), a survey item was used that asks each respondent who reported making a contact how many such contacts he or she has made in the last year. With those who said they had contacted the Action Center removed, the measure of non-Action Center contacting propensity is the sum of all these survey-reported contacts for each neighborhood divided by the number of survey respondents in the neighborhood (that is, survey-reported contacts per respondent).

Consistent with the Vedlitz, Dyer, and Durand-style hypothesis, Action Center contacting shows a strong and statistically significant negative association (r = −.41; sig. = .024) with neighborhood social well-being, the latter measured by the value of owner-occupied housing; contacting propensity through other channels is much less strongly related to social well-being (r = −.22; sig. = .156). Scattergrams showing these relationships are provided in Figures 4-1 and 4-2. Figure 4-1 shows that neighborhoods at the low end of the social well-being scale generate much higher volumes of contacts to the Action Center than do neighborhoods at the high end of the scale. Most notably, the three neighborhoods with extremely high values on Action Center contacting propensity are all at the lowest extreme of the social well-being scale. This pattern replicates that found by Vedlitz, Dyer, and Durand (1980) in Dallas and Houston. Contacts to city council members, department heads, and other city officials are quite another matter (see Figure 4-2). Although contacting propensity diminishes somewhat as social well-being increases, the differences are not dramatic.

As noted above, Vedlitz, Dyer, and Durand (1980) speculate that the different patterns may emerge because centralized complaint units have a leveling effect on awareness. This leaves need as the major explanatory factor for contacts targeted to such units; and since need is inversely associated with social well-being, this explains the negative linear association between propensity to contact centralized complaint units and neighborhood social well-being.

There is evidence for this interpretation in the Kansas City data. At the neighborhood level, perceived need[4] shows a strong, negative relationship with social well-being as measured by average housing value (r = −.688; sig. = .001). So far, the findings are totally in accord with Jones and colleagues' (1977) need-awareness model, which Vedlitz, Dyer, and Durand were attempting to replicate in their Dallas and Houston research.

The extent to which awareness is positively associated with social well-being depends, however, on the type of political

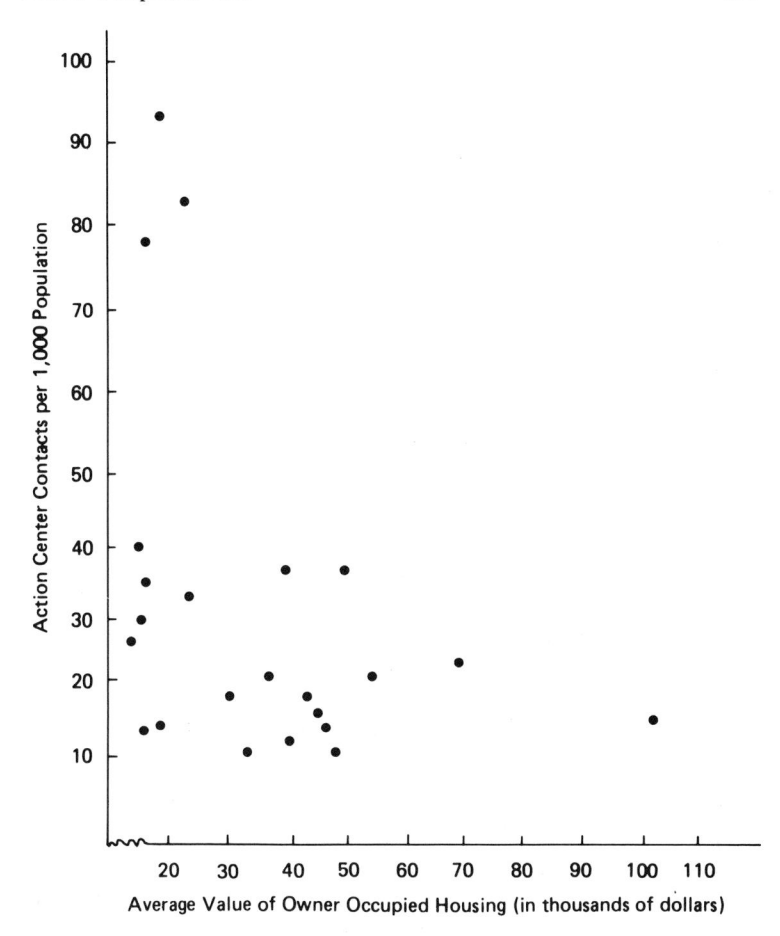

FIGURE 4-1. *Propensity to Contact the Action Center by Neighborhood Social Well-Being*

awareness at issue. Familiarity with key elected or appointed officials such as council members, the mayor, and the city manager[5] is strongly associated with area social well-being (r = .728; sig. = .001). Familiarity with Kansas City's Action Center,[6] however, shows a considerably weaker association with social well-being (r = .337; sig. = .054). This is precisely what

20   30   40   50   60   70   80   90   100   110

Average Value of Owner Occupied Housing (in thousands of dollars)

*Does not include Action Center contacts.

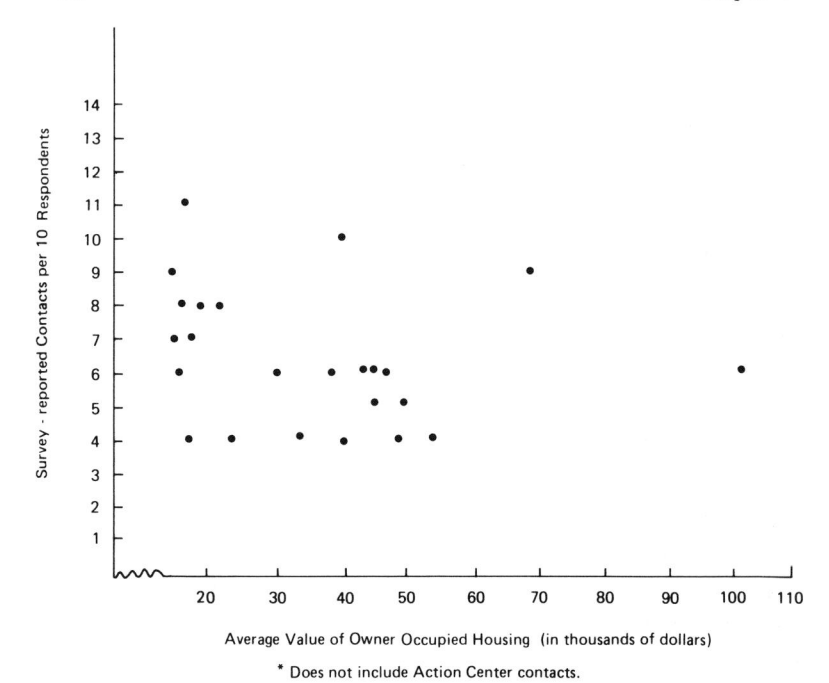

FIGURE 4-2. *Contacts with Officials Other than the Action Center, by Neighborhood Social Well-Being*

Vedlitz, Dyer, and Durand (1980) suggest. Awareness of this central complaints unit is much more evenly distributed than is awareness of public officials more generally. Consequently, Action Center contacting is more a function of neighborhood need than is contacting directed at other government officials.

We have seen that, although Kansas City's centralized complaints unit has not supplanted other channels of access to government, such a unit has an impact on neighborhood patterns of contact. Unlike other forms of political information, awareness of the Action Center is more evenly distributed across neighborhoods, so variations in Action Center contacting are primarily a function of neighborhood need.

If political sophistication about other channels of access were distributed as evenly as awareness of the Action Center, the overall pattern of demands upon city government could be as much a function of need as is Action Center contacting. Political awareness is strikingly unequally distributed, however, and for this reason, demand-making that is not funneled through the Action Center is not very respresentative of neighborhood need.

Citizen Satisfaction with Government's Response to Contacts

To understand fully what difference a central complaints unit makes, we must consider not only the volume of contacts received and the social geography of contacting propensity, but also citizens' assessments of how their contacts were handled. As Eisinger notes, contacting is a "demand for representation in that the contactor asks in effect that an official act on behalf of his concerns" (1972: 43). If a central complaints unit such as the Action Center is no better or worse at handling such demands than the mayor, a council member, or a department official, then the existence of such central units cannot be said to make much difference in the quality of life of urban residents.

All respondents who had contacted a local government official were asked to evaluate the response to their request or complaint on three criteria: promptness, effectiveness, and courtesy. Specifically, they were asked: (1) How would you rate the promptness of the person or agency in dealing with your complaint or request? (2) How good was the person or agency about doing what needed to be done about your request or complaint? (3) How would you rate the courtesy of the person that you contacted?

Table 4-4 shows responses to these items, broken down by the target of the citizen's contact. People who contact the Action Center were, overall, the most satisfied with the handling of their requests, perhaps especially with respect to the promptness with which inquiries were handled. Not surprisingly, those who simply called city hall were consistently the least satisfied. The citizen who simply calls city hall presumably knows no more appropriate, specific channel of access and must therefore rely upon the capacity and good graces of the switchboard operator to determine the nature of the problem and refer the caller to the appropriate agency. Table 4-4 suggests that such an approach is ultimately not very satisfactory.

The closest competitors of the Action Center in these evaluation ratings are elected officials (mayor, council members). Although very few citizens took their problems to these elected officials, those who did were as prone to give excellent ratings on promptness as were those who contacted the Action Center; and the proportion giving excellent ratings on courtesy was even higher than among those who contacted the Action Center. Interestingly, however, those who contacted elected officials apparently did not find them to be particularly effective in getting problems resolved.

No information is available on the orientation of elected officials in Kansas City toward their "constituency casework" role, but there is no reason to believe that these officials are peculiarly disinclined to pursue such activity. Indeed, citizens' ratings of their courtesy and promptness suggest that officials make an effort, but the results are less satisfactory than when the Action Center handles the problems. It is possible, of course, that citizens take more difficult problems to elected officials whereas the Action Center receives more routine, easily resolvable problems. Such a scenario would explain the contrasting effectiveness ratings in Table 4-4. There is, however, no evidence available to substantiate this possibility.

It is at least as likely that elected officials are less effective in responding to demands (at least in the eyes of the citizen involved) because they do not have the resources that the Action Center does to goad the bureaucracy into action. Most problems or requests that citizens make ultimately require action on the part of one of the regular operating departments of city government.

TABLE 4-4. *Evaluations of Government Response to Contact by Target of Contact (percentages)*

Promptness Rating	Target of Contact				
	Action Center	Elected	Specific Dept.	City Hall	Other
Excellent	49	44	24	22	30
Good	28	24	28	17	17
Acceptable	7	16	14	19	17
Poor	10	4	19	20	16
Unacceptable	6	12	15	22	20
	100	100	100	100	100
(N)	(71)	(25)	(270)	(81)	(70)

Raw Chi^2 = 38.477   Significance = .001

Effectiveness Rating	Target of Contact				
	Action Center	Elected	Specific Dept.	City Hall	Other
Excellent	41	24	24	15	29
Good	27	20	26	30	23
Acceptable	19	20	12	21	13
Poor	9	12	16	16	17
Unacceptable	4	24	22	18	17
	100	100	100	100	99
(N)	(68)	(25)	(272)	(81)	(69)

Raw Chi^2 = 29.092   Significance = .023

Courtesy Rating	Target of Contact				
	Action Center	Elected	Specific Dept.	City Hall	Other
Excellent	48	56	35	24	41
Good	39	26	40	44	32
Acceptable	12	0	16	24	21
Poor	0	11	6	5	3
Unacceptable	1	7	3	3	3
	100	100	100	100	100
(N)	(69)	(27)	(267)	(79)	(66)

Raw Chi^2 = 29.781   Significance = .019

In Kansas City, department personnel are appointed, evaluated, promoted, and fired in a chain of command that ends with the city manager's office; in this reform-style government, elected officials have no direct powers over the city bureaucracy. The Action Center is a part of the city manager's office, and records of departmental response to problems forwarded through the Action Center are used in evaluations of department heads.

These institutional arrangements give the Action Center considerable leverage over operating departments that must deliver if citizens' problems are to be resolved; elected officials do not have these forms of leverage. Even if it were not for these particular institutional arrangements, there is reason to believe that operating departments are not readily nudged into action by elected officials. Kenneth Greene (1982) found, in a study of public officials in New Jersey municipalities, that most department officials do not believe that it is appropriate for elected officials to contact administrators on behalf of constituents. In general, Greene found that "administrators are more desirous of avoiding elected officials' contacts than cooperating with them" (1982: 6). Furthermore, this is particularly true of "professional-technocratic" administrators—those who believe that decisions regarding service delivery should be made on the basis of specialized knowledge and the technical criteria embodied in professional standards. It is highly likely that, in the reform-style government of Kansas City, operating departments are largely populated with professional-technocrats rather than politicos; if so, this would reinforce prevailing resistance to elected officials' efforts to get things done for constituents.

In this line of discussion, operating departments have been cast in the role of the heavy. They are ultimately the units that must act if citizens' complaints and requests are to be resolved, yet we appear to be assuming that they will not act appropriately unless some leverage is applied—leverage that the Action Center can apply more successfully than can elected officials.

This is not meant to demean the competence or good intentions of the personnel of urban service delivery agencies. The problem arises because such agencies operate in accordance with bureaucratic decision rules (Jones, et al., 1978; Levy, Meltsner, and Wildavsky, 1974) that are based on professional, technocratic standards and geared toward organizational imperatives. In some cases, agencies operate under decision rules that orient them toward responsiveness to citizens' requests, as when "Adam Smith" rules (Levy, Meltsner, and Wildavsky, 1974) are the order of the day. Even if an agency uses a decision rule of delivering services on demand, however, responsiveness is not guaranteed. "Adam Smith" rules do not mean that the agency responds to all requests, but to appropriate requests, and the agency's definition of appropriate may differ from the citizen's.

Furthermore, although "Adam Smith" rules are widespread, they are not the only operational form of bureaucratic decision rules. Frank Levy, Arnold Meltsner, and Aaron Wildavsky (1974) document a variety of other decision rules that may make urban service delivery agencies appear less than responsive to certain segments of the community.

For all these reasons, even well-intentioned, professional urban bureaucracies are likely to disappoint citizens on many occasions. Table 4-4 documents that this is the case. Citizens who contacted a specific city department directly were more dissatisfied with the promptness, effectiveness, and courtesy with which their problems were handled than any other group except those who simply called city hall. Indeed, it is because of the difficulties that citizens may encounter in approaching operating departments directly that many cities have instituted centralized complaints units to act as mediating bodies between the citizen and the bureaucracy and to spur the bureaucracy's response to the citizen.

There is evidence that, at least to some extent, Kansas Citians who use the Action Center understand this mediating role. A debriefing questionnaire was sent to a random sample[7] of citizens who had recently used the Action Center. The brief, postcard questionnaire asked these citizens to rate the quality of the service provided, to indicate whether they would again be willing to use the Action Center, and to provide an assessment of the overall responsiveness of Kansas City government. The quantitative results of this debriefing survey are perhaps less interesting[8] than the comments that many respondents scrawled on the postcard or wrote in letters to accompany the postcard.

For example, one respondent, who signed herself "A Determined Citizen," explained: "I have contacted Action Center on two separate occasions. Action Center has always been quick to act but the agencies contacted by Action Center tend to drag their feet. Example: Systematic and Environmental Inspections. I will say that when I reported Animal Control to Action Center that results from this complaint were immediate, Animal Control was out in my area within three days versus never when I contacted Animal Control on my own." Another respondent wrote: "I feel I shouldn't have *had* to call Action [Center] to get any response but once I did I got response. No complaint with Action Center." Even when respondents ultimately did not get problems resolved satisfactorily, there is evidence that judgment of the Action Center is distinguished from judgment of operating agencies, as the following comments suggest: "Action Center does the best they can by reporting. The parties actually carrying out the services stink." "I like the Action Center. But they can't install the lights we need. All they do is report a request." A citizen who assumed the postcard questionnaire was sent by the Action Center wrote, "Your action was okay—but the response from the trash department was just an excuse. There is still trash all over the neighborhood."

These voluntary comments from a sample of Action Center users cannot, of course, be taken as definitive evidence that most Kansas Citians understand and appreciate the mediating role of the Action Center. But the comments suggest that some sense of this role is percolating through the community, as is also clear in the comment of the Southton Neighborhood Association leader who noted: "[We have found] through a decade of experience that, if you go directly to a department, your request dies; but because the Action Center requires a report from the department and sends an evaluation card, you get something if you work with them." In short, although the Action Center is not always able to get satisfactory results for the citizen from the bureaucracy, there is at least some recognition that it is a better bet than approaching city departments directly. The Action Center's high ratings can be sustained if citizens distinguish its brokering role from the operating departments' ultimate service delivery role. Disappointment with the departments does not then necessarily translate into dissatisfaction with the Action Center.

Perceptions of Government Responsiveness

Citizens' evaluations of how their problems were handled are important in and of themselves because they provide the best available evidence of the quality of the Action Center's handling of contacts relative to that of other agencies or officials. Although there has been considerable debate about the value of such citizen satisfaction measures as indicators of actual performance (Stipak, 1979; Hatry, et al., 1977; Fitzgerald and Durant, 1980), it is difficult to deny their relevance. The dominant paradigm of city government (Sharp, 1980b) treats the city as a service-providing entity, different from private-sector providers in financing but pursuing a similar goal of customer satisfaction.

From a larger perspective, evaluations of how well contacts are handled are important if they have an impact on broader citizen attitudes toward the local political system. A disappointed contactor is one thing—an alienated citizen is quite another. In particular, the citizen's perception of government responsiveness is usually considered an important political attitude and an important predictor of a variety of political behaviors (Yates, 1977; Greenstone and Peterson, 1973). I will address this matter at greater length in the following chapter. Here it is important to consider whether citizens' reactions to the demand-making experience are linked to more general views on government responsiveness.

There is considerable evidence on this point, both for contactors in general and Action Center contactors in particular. Tables 4-5 and 4-6 show the relationships between evaluation of contact response and perception of local government responsiveness for all respondents to the citizen survey who reported having con-

TABLE 4-5. *Perceptions of Government Responsiveness (I) by Ratings of How Well Contact was Handled*

	Promptness Rating				
	Excellent	Good	Acceptable	Poor	Unacceptable
Kansas City government does *not* try to provide services wanted (percent)	6	12	15	27	25
(N)	(151)	(131)	(78)	(85)	(80)

Gamma = .41
Kendall's Tau_b = .19
Pearson's r = .21   Sig. < .001

	Effectiveness Rating				
	Excellent	Good	Acceptable	Poor	Unacceptable
Kansas City government does *not* try to provide services wanted (percent)	9	8	13	30	25
(N)	(133)	(144)	(77)	(81)	(90)

Gamma = .39
Kendall's Tau_b = .18
Pearson's r = .21   Sig. < .001

	Courtesy Rating				
	Excellent	Good	Acceptable	Poor	Unacceptable
Kansas City government does *not* try to provide services wanted (percent)	10	13	19	38	44
(N)	(186)	(200)	(88)	(24)	(16)

Gamma = .35
Kendall's Tau_b = .16
Pearson's r = .20   Sig. < .001

Central Complaints Unit

tacted a government official. In Table 4-5, attitude about government responsiveness is measured by a yes-no survey item asking: Do you think that Kansas City government tries to provide the kinds of services that people in your neighborhood want? In Table 4-6, attitude toward government responsiveness is assessed by a survey item asking: How responsive are local government offi-

TABLE 4-6. *Perceptions of Government Responsiveness (II) by Ratings of How Well Contact was Handled*

	Promptness Rating				
	Excellent	Good	Acceptable	Poor	Unacceptable
Not at all responsive (percent)	2	7	0	11	22
(N)	(135)	(122)	(76)	(90)	(78)
	Gamma = .44				
	Kendall's Tau_b = .32				
	Pearson's r = .37 Sig. < .001				

	Effectiveness Rating				
	Excellent	Good	Acceptable	Poor	Unacceptable
Not at all responsive (percent)	2	3	6	13	17
(N)	(117)	(133)	(78)	(82)	(90)
	Gamma = .44				
	Kendall's Tau_b = .32				
	Pearson's r = .37 Sig. < .001				

	Courtesy Rating				
	Excellent	Good	Acceptable	Poor	Unacceptable
Not at all responsive (percent)	4	5	9	19	39
(N)	(167)	(193)	(90)	(26)	(13)
	Gamma = .40				
	Kendall's Tau_b = .27				
	Pearson's r = .31 Sig. < .001				

cials to your concerns? Response categories for the latter item are "very," "somewhat," "slightly," and "not at all." Both tables report the percentages of respondents believing government to be nonresponsive.

Regardless of the measure of responsiveness used, there are relatively strong associations between ratings of how the individual's contact was handled and beliefs about government responsiveness. Those giving unacceptable ratings on promptness, for example, were four times as likely as those giving excellent ratings to say that Kansas City government does not try to provide the services people in the neighborhood want (see Table 4-5). The same is true of courtesy ratings; and those giving unacceptable ratings on effectiveness were almost three times as likely as those giving excellent ratings to say that Kansas City does not try to provide the services people in the neighborhood want. The differences in Table 4-6 are, if anything, more dramatic. Those giving unacceptable ratings on promptness, for example, were about ten times as likely as those giving excellent ratings to say that local officials are not at all responsive; the same is true of courtesy ratings.

The conclusion to be drawn from these responses is that citizens do generalize from their direct experience with city government. If government fails them when they take the initiative to make a demand, they are likely to develop a more jaundiced view of local government. As sensible as this conclusion may seem, it might be challenged by those arguing that cause-effect relationships cannot be conclusively demonstrated with cross-sectional analysis of this type. At least two alternative interpretations are possible. One is that the causal sequence implied in Tables 4-5 and 4-6 should be reversed. That is, perhaps it is not so much that citizens generalize from their direct experiences to their overall views of city government but that they "specifize." Hence the data could be interpreted as revealing that general attitudes toward government are displaced onto evaluations of specific experiences. A second interpretation would offer the proximity of the two measures—ratings of government responsiveness and ratings of how contacts were handled are asked for in a single survey instrument—as a point at issue. Presumably, respondents might bring their responsiveness item answers into accord with what they have told the interviewer about how government handled their contact (the responsiveness items were asked toward the end of the survey; the evaluation of the contacting experience occurred toward the beginning).

Although it is difficult to respond to the first of these alternative interpretations, evidence is available with respect to the second. Debriefing questionnaires were sent to a sample of recent Action Center users. Both government responsiveness items (see Tables 4-5 and 4-6) were incorporated in this debriefing questionnaire, as was a summary rating of the quality with which the respondents' contacts were handled—a rating that parallels those used on the general citizen survey.[9]

If this were the only information available, we could be no more sure of the conclusions than with those from the general citizen survey, for in the debriefing questionnaire respondents were also asked to evaluate both overall government responsiveness and government's handling of their particular contact within the same questionnaire. But this is not the only information available. The Action Center itself sends each contactor a postcard asking for an evaluation of how well the problem was handled. The postcard is sent as soon as the case is closed. When recent Action Center contactors were sampled for debriefing purposes, the Action Center's case number was recorded for each respondent. Consequently, the debriefing questionnaires from this study could be matched up with the postcards returned to the Action Center with citizens' evaluations at the time their cases were closed. These Action Center postcards were not always available (the Action Center's response rate is a little more than 40 percent), but they were available for a little over half of the debriefing questionnaires returned for this study.

The significance of the Action Center postcard evaluations is that they provide a measure of citizens' evaluations of how their contacts were handled that is separate in time and context from citizens' assessments of overall government responsiveness on the debriefing questionnaire. As Table 4-7 shows, this separation does make a difference. The link between assessment of how one's contact was handled and belief about government responsiveness is much higher when the measure of the former is drawn from the debriefing instrument than when it is drawn from a postcard that the citizen has returned to the Action Center before ever seeing my debriefing questionnaire.

There is, in other words, merit in the argument that citizens bring their global evaluations of government responsiveness into line with their specific assessments of their demand-making experiences. Nevertheless, there is still a substantial association between evaluation of the contacting experience and perception of government responsiveness, even when measures of the two are drawn from different instruments administered at different times (see panels 1b and 2b of Table 4-7). At least for this subset of Action Center contactors, we can be reassured that the association between evaluation of the contacting experience and perception of government responsiveness is not merely a methods artifact; nor is there any obvious reason to believe that other contactors would be any different were we to have a parallel, independent source of information about their evaluations of the contacting experience.

This analysis of Kansas City's Action Center is intended to provide some assessment of the impact such a centralized complaint-handling unit has. One cannot say, of course, whether every city that institutes a central complaints unit would observe the same outcomes, but Kansas City's Action Center is exemplary of the administrative ombudsman approach common in this country. The results observed here are not, therefore, likely to be completely idiosyncratic, although they may be most applicable to cities with a "reform"-style government structure.

Kansas City's central complaints unit is, in some respects, a disappointment. Most notably, it does not serve as the primary channel of access to city government for problem-solving, either for the citizenry as a whole or for disadvantaged subgroups in particular. At one level, this shortcoming would seem to be small grounds for disappointment. The Action Center does appear to be serving various socioeconomic groups about equally, which cannot be said of every urban institution. There is evidence that minority citizens do not make heavier use of the Action Center because they find other avenues of access to city government to be preferable, largely because of the nonpolitical nature of the Action Center and its orientation toward individual problem-solving rather than resource-allocation issues. Thus the Action Center cannot be said to have failed to serve any particular group; rather, it has simply not replaced other avenues for citizen-initiated contacting.

Yet the surprisingly small proportion of Kansas City residents who engage in demand-making via the Action Center is disappointing because apparent potential has been lost. At the neighborhood level, Action Center contacting is much more a function of neighborhood need than is contacting via other channels, largely because political sophistication about channels of access generally is much more unevenly distributed according to social well-being than is awareness of the Action Center. Because many urban services are distributed on the basis of demand, service distribution would be better geared to need if demand-making overall followed the Action Center pattern.

Furthermore, we find that citizens are much more satisfied with the handling of their contacts made to the Action Center than to other agencies. Most citizens take their problems directly to the operating departments involved; but these citizens are much less likely to provide favorable ratings for promptness, effectiveness, and courtesy than are those who depend on the Action Center as an intermediary. In short, the Action Center holds a potential for greater citizen satisfaction that is not fully realized so long as citizens rely upon other avenues of access to city government.

Enhancing citizens' satisfaction with the handling of their complaints and requests is more than an empty exercise in boosting performance evaluations. There is evidence that citizens' evaluations of their experiences with city government are linked to broader beliefs about the responsiveness of local government.

TABLE 4-7. *Perceptions of Government Responsiveness by Evaluation of How Contact Was Handled (Action Center Debriefees)*

	\multicolumn{4}{c}{Rating of How Well Contact Handled (Debriefing Survey)}
	Excellent	Good	Acceptable	Poor	Unacceptable

1a) Kansas City government does not try to provide services wanted

| (percent) | 8 | 12 | 33 | 53 | 75 |
| (N) | (86) | (91) | (42) | (17) | (24) |

Gamma = .68
Kendall's Tau$_b$ = .39
Pearson's r = .48   Sig. < .001

	\multicolumn{4}{c}{Rating of How Well Contact Handled (Action Center card)}
	Excellent	Good	Acceptable	Poor	Unacceptable

1b) Kansas City government does not try to provide services wanted

| (percent) | 10 | 16 | 20 | 25 | 55 |
| (N) | (61) | (44) | (10) | (8) | (11) |

Gamma = .47
Kendall's Tau$_b$ = .23
Pearson's r = .30   Sig. < .01

	Rating of How Well Contact Handled (Debriefing Survey)			
	Excellent	Good	Acceptable	Poor	Unacceptable
2a) Local officials are only slightly or not at all responsive (percent)	10	13	48	45	83
(N)	(89)	(93)	(42)	(18)	(24)

Gamma = .67
Kendall's Tau$_b$ = .51
Pearson's r = .60   Sig. < .001

	Rating of How Well Contact Handled (Action Center card)			
	Excellent	Good	Acceptable	Poor	Unacceptable
2b) Local officials are only slightly or not at all responsive (percent)	11	16	30	38	45
(N)	(64)	(43)	(10)	(8)	(11)

Gamma = .46
Kendall's Tau$_b$ = .32
Pearson's r = .34   Sig. < .001

There may be important, longer-run consequences if disappointment with service delivery and the demand-making experience translates not only into a generalized discontent with city government but also a propensity to "exit." The following chapter explores this issue.

The Need Awareness and Socioeconomic Models: A Pause to Take Stock

From the outset, a pair of contrasting explanatory models has provided the springboard for analysis of citizen-initiated contacting for urban services. The models offer contradictory predictions about patterns of citizen-initiated contacting, but they have been devised and tested from different methodological standpoints—that is, individual versus aggregate spatial units of analysis and survey-reported versus agency-recorded data. This difference has provided two challenges for the analysis at hand: (1) to determine whether conflicting findings are merely artifacts of different methodologies, and (2) to attempt a synthesis of the two explanatory models. Chapters 2, 3, and 4 represent some progress on these two fronts. This section provides a summary of that progress.

The need-awareness model, for example, has been tested, using an approach more typical of the socioeconomic model—analysis of individuals rather than spatial units and use of survey rather than agency data. The results are mixed. Although need emerges as a key explanatory factor, the overall model does not work as specified. Most notably, a curvilinear pattern of contacting, with propensity highest at the middle range of social well-being, does not emerge.

We need not conclude, however, that the success of the need-awareness model is therefore contingent on the methodology of application. Other, more interesting reasons for the mixed results have been uncovered. These include (1) the possibility that different socioeconomic subgroups have different threshold levels of need and awareness; (2) the significance of contextual factors not encompassed by the original need-awareness model—most notably activity of neighborhood organizations; and (3) the leveling effect that a centralized complaints unit can have upon citizens' awareness relevant to the contacting process. Apart from these, the need-awareness model might be expected to work better as originally formulated than it does when survey-based data are used because the original formulation relies upon objective measures of need, whereas the survey approach suggests the importance of perceived need. Objective need shows the strong, inverse associations with social well-being variables that the need-awareness model posits, but perceived need shows only very modest inverse associations with those variables.

Similarly, when adapted to the sort of neighborhood-level analysis from which the need-awareness model was derived, the socioeconomic model does not work. Instead, agency-recorded (Action Center) contacts are highest in areas that are lowest on the social well-being scale. Again, however, there is something more interesting at work than methodology driving results. What is most notable about the negative association in Figure 4-1 is its consistency with the pattern that Vedlitz, Dyer, and Durand (1980) found in Dallas and Houston—a pattern that appears to be characteristic of communities with central complaint-handling units. In short, such units may, at least within the narrow realm of matters within their purview, diminish the socioeconomic differences in awareness that are found in other aspects of local political life. The weakness of the socioeconomic model, in other words, is at least in part a function of local institutional arrangements that are designed to overcome the very patterns that the socioeconomic model outlines.

Furthermore, the socioeconomic model does not perform particularly well even when tested at the individual level with survey data. As Chapter 2 showed, this is largely because the role of mediating political attitudes and competencies that the model posits is problematic. Knowledge of and interest in government are not of compelling importance as precursors of demand-making, although a sense of political efficacy is; and, although there are substantial socioeconomic differences in local political knowledge, neither political efficacy nor interest in government is a function of socioeconomic status.

In short, Chapters 2, 3 and 4 suggest neither that one of the models definitively preempts the other, nor that the outcomes of each are driven by the methodology entailed. They suggest instead some important reasons for the limitations of each and an important avenue for synthesis. That synthesis involves more than the selection of the best of the predictor variables from each model, although efficacy, perceived need, and education alone carry us a reasonable distance toward explaining contacting propensity. Synthesis must also entail attention to the context in which citizen-initiated contacting occurs. Individuals' propensity to engage in this form of demand-making depends not only upon their own socioeconomic status but also upon the interaction between their status and the social context of their neighborhood. It depends not only upon objective need in the neighborhood but also upon the activities of neighborhood organizations, which sometimes encourage the translation of need into demands and sometimes do not. And it depends upon whether there is a centralized complaints unit that has been able to even out socioeconomic differences in political awareness. In sum, understanding patterns of citizen-initiated contacting requires a contingency perspective, based on attention to the significantly different contexts in which demand-making can occur.

NOTES TO CHAPTER 4

1. About two-fifths (39.4 percent) of all respondents had heard of the Action Center and correctly described it. By way of comparison, 34 percent could name the city manager, 35 percent could name a council member, and 78 percent could name the mayor.

2. Here, as in previous chapters, pseudonyms rather than actual neighborhood names are used to protect the anonymity of neighborhood organization leaders who were interviewed.

3. Separate samples had to be drawn because open and closed cases are filed separately. A 50 percent random sample of closed cases and a 24 percent random sample of open cases were drawn. Each type was weighted according to its sampling percentage, and the two were added to derive the number of total expected Action Center contacts from each neighborhood.

4. The measure of need for this neighborhood-level analysis is the percentage of respondents in each neighborhood who rated more than one of the fourteen potential problem items as a big problem.

5. Knowledge of the Action Center is excluded from this measure of more traditional political awareness. The measure is built from the remaining four awareness items used in previous chapters—whether respondents could name the city manager, the mayor, their district council representative, and any other council member. For this neighborhood-level analysis, awareness is the average number of correct responses among the respondents for each neighborhood.

6. The measure of awareness of the Action Center is the proportion of respondents from each neighborhood who said they had heard of the Action Center and who correctly described it.

7. For the debriefing survey, conducted in June 1983, postcard questionnaires were sent out to every individual whose Action Center case had been closed within the preceding month, excluding business complainants and complainants without usable addresses. About 500 postcards were sent and 287 were returned, for a response rate of 57.4 percent.

8. Ratings of the quality of service provided were 34 percent "excellent," 35 percent "good," 15 percent "acceptable," 7 percent "poor," and 9 percent "unacceptable." Eighty-nine percent said they would be willing to use the Action Center again, 10 percent said they would contact someone else, and less than 1 percent said they wouldn't contact anyone if they had a similar problem in the future.

9. Because of limited space, respondents were not asked to rate promptness, effectiveness, and courtesy separately, as respondents to the general citizen survey were. Instead, respondents were simply asked, Please rate the service recently provided (if any) in response to your request. The response categories are the same as those in the promptness, effectiveness, and courtesy items on the general survey. The two government responsiveness items on the debriefing instrument are identical to those used in the general citizen survey. On the debrief-

ing survey, 78 percent responded that Kansas City government does try to provide the services wanted, and 22 percent said that it does not; 42 percent rated local officials as very responsive, 33 percent rated them as somewhat responsive, 17 percent said they were slightly responsive, and 8 percent said they were not at all responsive.

5

Demand-Making and Mobility: Tiebout Revisited

☑ ☑ ☑
☑ ☑ ☐

At the height of the anti–Vietnam war protests in this country, "America, Love It or Leave It" became the favorite slogan of those offended by the antiwar movement. Perhaps the slogan gained special popularity because of the irony that it captures. Although the slogan ostensibly expressed a choice, its users presumed that leaving would not be an appealing or viable option. Where could one go that would be preferable? "Leaving it," in short, was viewed as only an ironic option.

The mobility option is relevant in the urban context, however, and it has been taken seriously by students of urban affairs. Suburbanization and the deconcentration of central cities, more recent evidence that young, upwardly mobile professionals (or "Yuppies" in popular parlance) are returning to "gentrify" pockets of the inner city, and the comparative growth of "sunbelt" cities relative to the "frostbelt" are mobility phenomena that occupy center stage in discussions of urban politics and development.

Mobility, in the residential relocation sense, obviously is a key component of urban growth and decline. But to what extent is mobility linked to the urban services that city governments provide and citizens' evaluations of those services? We have seen in the last chapter that citizens' evaluations of the overall responsiveness of local government are greatly influenced by their experiences with government in citizen-initiated contacting situations. This suggests that citizen demand-making about urban

133

services and the character of government's response to those demands have significant implications for the general orientation of citizens to their local government. This chapter considers the possibility that there are perhaps more serious implications of citizens' discontent with urban government's performance—that is, that dissatisfied citizens use residential relocation as a device to escape from unsatisfactory local government. The role of citizen-initiated contacting, either as an alternative to this escape behavior or as a trigger of this behavior if government's response is not satisfactory, is a central focus of this chapter.

It is possible, however, that the residential location calculus is dominated by concerns of family cycle, housing characteristics, and access to jobs, with little consideration for the quantity or quality of public services existing in various locations. If this were the case, neither the character of urban public services nor city government's response to citizen demand-making with respect to urban services would be of much relevance for understanding mobility and patterns of urban growth and decline. Our first task, therefore, is to consider the theoretical linkages between urban government's performance, citizen demand-making, and mobility. Several important perspectives condition current thinking about these issues. They are briefly reviewed here.

Tiebout's "Pure Theory of Local Expenditures"

Urban public services and taxes are critically important considerations in the residential location calculus, according to Tiebout's (1956) classic formulation. In this analysis, the importance of public services and taxes is not compared to that of other relocation factors, such as job availability. Rather, Tiebout (1956: 422) simply strives to show deductively that "spatial mobility provides the local public-goods counterpart to the private market's shopping trip." Written at a time when social scientists were first reacting to the implications of the postwar suburbanization boom, Tiebout's article stresses (1956: 420) that "every resident who moves to the suburbs to find better schools, more parks, and so forth is reacting, in part, against the pattern the city has to offer."

Perhaps most important, Tiebout formulates a model of residential mobility in which citizens are acting to maximize the realization of a set of urban service and tax preferences. Given the multiplicity of local government jurisdictions in the metropolitan area, Tiebout offers the theoretical possibility that an optimal allocation of services and taxes across the metropolitan area, corresponding to the equilibrium point of the competitive market model, can be achieved. It is important, however, that in this metropolitan marketplace in which jurisdictions offer various bundles of services and taxes the choices and decisions are made by the consumer-resident: "The act of moving or failing to move is crucial. Moving or failing to move replaces the usual market test of willingness to buy a good and reveals the consumer-voters' demand for public goods" (Tiebout, 1956: 420). Local governments, however, do not make decisions in response to market forces according to this formulation: "At the central level the preferences of the consumer-voter are given and the government tries to adjust to the pattern of these preferences, whereas at the local level various governments have their revenue and expenditure patterns more or less set. Given these revenue and expenditure patterns, the consumer-voter moves to that community whose local government best satisfies his set of preferences" (Tiebout, 1956: 420).

Tiebout thus offers a perspective in which urban services and taxes are a critical part of the residential location calculus; but mobility is the only citizen-consumer response considered. Citizens, in this model, register their preference "with their feet" rather than through voting, citizen-initiated contacting, or other modes of political participation. Similarly, local governments, in this formulation, are not in a responsive posture; rather, they offer whatever service-tax bundle is set by prevailing circumstances in the community and then either suffer or enjoy, as the case may be, the results of ensuing mobility patterns.

Tiebout's analysis has perhaps been most influential in crystallizing, through the metaphor of "voting with one's feet," the ongoing debate over the desirability of prevailing patterns of local government organization in metropolitan areas. Specifically, a Tiebout-style perspective characterizes the work of public choice theorists who criticize suggestions for metropolitan consolidation (Bish and Ostrom, 1973), fiscal equalization (Bish, 1976), and other reforms that are offered on the presumption that metropolitan "fragmentation" necessarily has unwholesome consequences.

Many critics of "fragmented" local government in metropolitan areas also accept the Tiebout hypothesis that citizen-consumers "vote with their feet" to obtain their preferred package of services and taxes. These critics see pernicious effects from this dynamic, rather than the market equilibrium of Tiebout's original formulation. Some, such as James O'Connor (1973), emphasize the way in which the metropolitan marketplace leaves impoverished central cities, dominated by their suburbs in a manner analogous to imperial domination of colonies. Accepting Tiebout's thesis that preferences can be expressed through family mobility, O'Connor (1973: 126–27) concludes that "class conflict which in an earlier period sharply divided the city, finally was placed on a metropolitan basis."

These inequalities and the resulting metropolitan organization of class conflict are said to arise because of the differential mobility of different social groups in the metropolitan area, which is exacerbated by the devices used by privileged classes to close off the metropolitan marketplace after they have made their choices: "Local jurisdictions with better-off residents use their governing powers to control access to scarce resources and to insulate themselves against land uses of migrations of low-income individuals whose economic class or public-service needs would increase the burden of supporting public services" (Neiman, 1982: 220).

Although there has been considerable ferment about this metropolitan question, there is little conclusive evidence concerning

Demand-Making and Mobility

some of the key assumptions underlying the debate, especially the Tiebout-like assumption that residential location hinges upon the public service–tax packages offered by various jurisdictions. Ironically, two traditions (public choice and the critics of metropolitan fragmentation) that are otherwise vociferously opposed appear equally willing to accept the assumption and to forge on with debate about consequences.

There are some exceptions, of course. For example, a recent analysis (Schneider and Logan, 1982) indirectly tested the Tiebout hypothesis by examining suburban growth rates in relation to government expenditures and tax rates. They found that neither expenditures nor tax rates were related to growth rates of either low-income or high-income families, an apparent refutation of the Tiebout hypothesis. Rather, tax base appears to be an important factor. Their research shows that "affluent families tended to concentrate in communities with stronger local property tax bases, while the poor tended to be excluded from such communities" (1982: 102)—a finding that is supportive of the metropolitan class inequalities perspective noted above. Similarly, Janet Pack (1973), Richard Cebula (1974), and Terry Clark and Lorna Ferguson (1983) have found that higher taxes are negatively associated with net population growth or net inmigration.

Apart from some research on welfare expenditures and migration patterns of the poor (Chao and Renas, 1976; Glantz, 1975), research linking service levels or quality to residential choice is more scarce, presumably because measuring variation in tax burden across jurisdictions is more straightforward than assessing variation in quality of urban services (but see Jackson, 1975). The latter is, however, more relevant in the context of a discussion of citizen-initiated contacting and mobility.

Furthermore, research on the Tiebout model usually does not directly test the core element of the model—the notion that mobility is linked to public service and tax preferences. Mark Schneider and John Logan acknowledge this shortcoming:

Our use of data on aggregate community development patterns precludes firm conclusions about the motivations for residential location choices by high-income or low-income households. Like most other work on the Tiebout model, which also uses aggregate data, we assume that differences among communities are perceived and enter into the decision calculus of movers. Yet, the test of the implicit inferences concerning the causal process linking local finances to growth patterns and the location decisions of individuals will ultimately require further research, most likely using survey methods. [1982: 97]

Survey data that permit this more direct assessment of Tiebout's assumption are introduced later in this chapter.

Hirschman's Typology of "Exit, Voice, and Loyalty"

Hirschman's (1970) analysis does not focus exclusively on the question of urban services and residential mobility. It deals with the more general question of the responses of individuals who are discontented with the services or activities of a firm, an organization, or a community. It is thus a more general formulation, which can be applied to the case at hand.

When so applied, Hirschman's analysis reminds us that mobility is only one of three possible responses for the discontented citizen-consumer. That is, mobility exemplifies the "exit" option—the dissatisfied customer or member can stop patronizing the offending firm, quit the organization, or leave the community that provides an unsatisfactory public service–tax bundle.

"Voice" is another option. That is, the discontented citizen, consumer, or member can complain or adopt any of a variety of tactics of political assertion designed to alter the prevailing and, from the citizen's perspective, undesirable pattern of outcomes. The distinction between the "exit" option and the "voice" option, as Hirschman acknowledges, is essentially one between the choice behavior of economic man and the influence attempts of political man. Finally, Hirschman reminds us that, in addition to

Demand-Making and Mobility

"exit" and "voice" the discontented citizen or consumer always has the option of "loyalty"—remaining a patron, member, or resident in the expectation that "*someone* will act or *something* will happen to improve matters" (1970: 78). Perhaps the most significant aspect of Hirschman's analysis, however, is its invitation to consider the trade-offs among the various options. The trade-offs between exit and voice are of special concern to Hirschman, and they have special relevance to the question of the impact of urban services on urban growth or decline. Essentially, Hirschman offers two possibilities: (1) the existence of the exit option can diminish voice, or (2) voice tends to be used as a first option, with exit as an option of last resort after voice has failed. Translated into the case at hand, there is concern that the capacity to move to another community or neighborhood provides an attractive escape from urban service problems, which makes it less likely that citizens will stay and engage in political pressure to force changes in urban government's service delivery policies.

Alternatively, an individual's potential mobility may not diminish political involvement. Political involvement, including demand-making through citizen-initiated contacting of public officials, can be a first-stage response to problems with urban services, followed by exit only if government's response to demands is unsatisfactory.

Surprisingly few direct, empirical tests have been done of Hirschman's alternative hypotheses concerning the relationship between exit and voice. The typology itself (exit, voice, and loyalty) has been the more influential aspect of Hirschman's work. John Orbell and Toru Uno (1972) however, applied a Hirschman-style analysis to data from Columbus, Ohio, and showed that the relationship of exit to voice is contingent upon individual and contextual variables. For example, the modal response to neighborhood problems for high-status residents of urban areas is voice and exit, which implies that for them exit is an option of last resort after voice; for low-status residents of urban areas, however, the modal response is exit without voice

(Orbell and Uno, 1972: 480). Similarly, Sharp (1984a), drawing from a Department of Housing and Urban Development national sample survey, reported that the relationship between exit and voice is contingent on the individual's social status (that is, education level). Among less-educated individuals, there is evidence that exit diminishes voice—those who are moving are much less likely to have engaged in the form of demand-making of special interest here (contacting government officials) than are those who are not planning to move. Among better-educated individuals, however, the exiters are just as prone to have engaged in demand-making before making their decision to move as are their non-mobile counterparts.

In short, although there has been relatively little empirical analysis of Hirschman's hypotheses, that which has been done suggests that mobility is more likely to diminish political participation among lower-social-status individuals; higher-status individuals appear to make use of both voice and exit. This finding is ironic in the light of the next major perspective on mobility and urban politics.

Peterson: The Politics of the "Limited City"

Like many others, Peterson (1981) in his influential book *City Limits,* accepts Tiebout's notion that family mobility is a function of the packages of public services and taxes available in various local jurisdictions. By focusing on the implications of this notion for jurisdictions at risk to lose taxpayers through the exit option, Peterson develops a framework for understanding the politics of the limited city—cities cannot control the national political economy of which they are a part nor can they control the migration of citizens as nation-states can. Rather than the metropolitan equilibrium modeled by Tiebout (in which the various local jurisdictions tend toward optimal sizes for service delivery and an optimal mix of tax and service packages results), Peterson describes a dynamic by which local governments actively shape

Demand-Making and Mobility 141

their own service and tax packages so as to avoid losing their higher-than-average taxpaying constituencies.

Ironically, however, Peterson's analysis can be viewed as minimizing the significance of basic urban service delivery with respect to mobility. To understand why this is so, it is important to note the distinctions made between the developmental, redistributive, and allocation policies of city government. Developmental policies are described as "local programs which enhance the economic position of a community in its competition with others . . . their positive economic effects are greater than their cost to community residents" (Peterson 1981: 41–42). The most obvious examples of such programs or services are industrial park development, other infrastructure improvements, tax concessions to business locating in the area, and the like. Peterson acknowledges that many of these programs entail costs as well as benefits and that expenditures for other purposes can enhance the competitive position of the community, but the general point is that one can identify a set of development-oriented expenditures designed to keep the community economically competitive and for which the benefit-tax ratio will be greater than 1.0 for the average taxpayer.

By contrast, Peterson characterizes a variety of redistributive policies as being "unproductive" from the standpoint of sustaining the community's economically competitive position: "Because redistributive policies help the needy and unfortunate and because they provide reasonably equal citizen access to public services, such policies are sometimes incorporated into local government practice, even when their economic consequences are pernicious . . . [but] redistributive programs have negative economic effects. While they supply benefits to those least needed by the local economy, they require taxation on those who are most needed" (1981: 43–44).

Finally, Peterson characterizes a host of the basic "housekeeping" services of local government, from fire and police protection to sanitation, as "allocational" policies that "have neither much of a positive nor much of a negative effect on the local economy" (1981: 44). Such services are important and valued by all segments of the community, but they "do not pay for themselves in the same way that developmental policies do." Consequently, the average and certainly the higher-than-average taxpaying citizens would be unlikely to reap marginal benefits from them that exceed marginal costs.

Peterson's thesis is that, because of the potential mobility of households (and firms, of course), all cities must be mindful of how their expenditure patterns, and resulting taxes, will affect their position in the competition among jurisdictions to hold the most "productive" constituents, with "productive" defined as contributing relatively more in taxes than service demands. Because of the competition among local jurisdictions, there is relatively little variation in tax rates across jurisdictions (Peterson, 1981: 46), an observation that may help to explain why Schneider and Logan (1982) did not find tax rate to be a significant factor in predicting growth of low- versus high-income populations in local jurisdictions.

Tax base, or fiscal capacity, does vary across jurisdictions, as do the costs of supplying services and the need for redistributive services. But given the assumption that cities need to stay competitive because of the potential mobility of productive segments of the community, Peterson concludes that developmental policies will have primacy, regardless of the city's fiscal capacity, whereas redistributive expenditures are constrained by the city's fiscal capacity. Regardless of need, cities will tend to spend only as much on redistributive programs as they can afford without losing a competitive tax rate. Basic housekeeping services occupy a middle ground in this model, and decision making about them is a function of fiscal capacity, demand, and supply costs (Peterson, 1981: 48-49).

In short, Peterson's thesis suggests that the real pressure points in the city's efforts to head off the exit of productive citizens involve trade-offs between redistributive and developmental policies. The basic housekeeping services of allocation politics do not loom as large in this analysis of what it takes for a city to sustain its competitive edge in the metropolitan marketplace. Yet the basic housekeeping services of local government—snow plowing, recreation, street maintenance, garbage collection, and the like—are by and large the stuff about which most citizen-initiated contacting revolves. Hence the trade-offs between voice and exit that are suggested by Hirschman's (1970) analysis invite consideration of this aspect of local government activity. Similarly, such basic housekeeping services are arguably essential components of the "service bundle" that citizens evaluate, according to the Tiebout model. Whether dissatisfaction with these basic housekeeping services is enough to drive taxpayers to exit, even if the city's developmental and redistributive policies are tailored to their concerns, is a question not directly addressed by Peterson.

Studies of Urban Mobility

Despite some differences in particulars and in focus, all of the perspectives examined so far are based on the assumption that family mobility is at least in part a response to the public service and tax decisions of urban governments. Against this backdrop, forms of demand-making such as citizen-initiated contacting take on added significance. Even cities that are sensitive to the mobility potential of taxpayers may not always generate decisions that are fully consistent with their preferences, particularly with regard to the host of matters encompassed within the politics of allocation. In Hirschman's terms, such communities need voice as a corrective mechanism; and to the extent that cities are responsive to the demands of citizens, there will presumably be less exit.

But how realistic are these perspectives from the standpoint of existing research on migration patterns and mobility? If Americans are not particularly mobile in the sense of relocating their place of residence, the exit option would have to be viewed as a relatively unimportant aspect of urban politics, and concerns about mobility as a response to dissatisfaction with urban services would seem overblown. Even if Americans are quite mobile, the Tiebout model and related perspectives are relevant only if there is evidence that local government services and taxes do loom large in the residential relocation calculus.

Americans are indeed mobile. For example, J. W. Simmons (1968: 622) reports that about 20 percent of the population changes residence each year and that 50 percent of the population changes residence in a five-year period. Nor is this a peculiarity of American society in the 1950s and 1960s. Leslie King and Reginald Golledge (1978: 314) report that "conservative estimates of intraurban mobility indicate that between 15 percent and 20 percent of urban populations in developed countries change their residence each year." Finally, Richard Dagger (1981: 726) notes that 41.3 percent of the population of the United States changed residence between 1970 and 1975.

These reports of census figures on actual mobility in the early 1970s can be compared with survey data on mobility plans in the late 1970s in the United States and a mobility item from the 1983 Kansas City survey. In a national sample survey conducted by Louis Harris and Associates in 1978 for the Department of Housing and Urban Development, respondents were asked: "Looking to the future for a moment, how likely are you to move in the next two or three years? Will you definitely move, probably move, probably not move, or definitely not move from this (house/apartment)?" Fifteen percent of those living in a larger or a medium-sized, nonsuburban city and 14 percent of those living in suburban communities said they definitely would move; another 20 percent of the former and 16 percent of the latter said they probably would move. A parallel question was included on the Kansas City survey, the only difference being that respondents were asked about their plans to move out of the neighborhood in the next year or two. Eight percent of the Kansas City respondents said they definitely would move out of the neighborhood, and 9 percent said they probably would do so.

The apparent lower mobility of Kansas City residents compared to the urbanites in the national sample HUD survey is to some extent an artifact of the slight differences in wording of the questions. This is more apparent when we consider a follow-up question from the HUD survey, which asked all definite or probable movers where they planned to move. Table 5-1 shows the results, again differentiating current urbanites from suburbanites. The boxed area of the table indicates categories of respondents that planned to leave their current neighborhood but remain in the United States. As the table indicates, 27.3 percent of the urbanites and 21.7 percent of the suburbanites planned such a move. Although the mobility gap between respondents to the 1983 Kansas City survey and these 1978 HUD survey respondents is narrowed when viewed in this light, there is still a noteworthy difference—only 17 percent of Kansas City respondents planned to move out of their neighborhoods in the near future. Whether this difference reflects peculiarities of the Kansas City area, the "next one or two years" time frame of the Kansas City item as compared to the "next two or three years" time frame of the HUD survey, or generally diminishing mobility in the 1980s (perhaps because of high mortgage rates or similar factors) cannot be determined from the data.

Table 5-1 also suggests another relevant issue for this analysis. Although more than one-third of the urbanites reported that they planned to move, clearly not all of these can be viewed as possible "Tiebout-ites," changing jurisdictions to obtain a more preferred tax and public service package. Only 19.8 percent of the urban respondents (or 57.2 percent of the urban movers) were planning to make a cross-jurisdictional move. Most of the other urbanites who were planning to move expected to relocate within the city in which they currently lived (the remainder either did not report a moving location or were planning to leave the country altogether).

This survey-based estimate of the proportion of urbanites planning a cross-jurisdictional move in the next two or three years is virtually identical to the estimate of cross-jurisdictional mobility that Dagger (1981) derived from Census Bureau data on actual

TABLE 5-1. *Moving Plans of a 1978 National Sample (percentages)*

	Residents of:	
	Big or Medium-Sized Nonsuburban Cities	Suburban Cities
Movers		
To		
Somewhere else in neighborhood	35.0	29.4
	4.0	5.3
Different neighborhood in this city	7.5 ⎫	2.9 ⎫
Suburb in this metropolitan area	4.0 ⎪	3.7 ⎪
Suburb outside this metro area	3.1 ⎬ 27.3	3.0 ⎬ 21.7
Different large city	3.9 ⎪	2.2 ⎪
Small city, town, or village	5.6 ⎪	6.3 ⎪
Rural area	3.2 ⎭	3.6 ⎭
Outside United States	1.1	--
Don't Know/Missing Data	2.6	2.4
Nonmovers	64.9	70.6
Totals	99.9	100.0
(N)	(2,904)	(2,066)

Source: Quality of Urban Life, a 1978 survey conducted by Louis Harris and Associates for the Department of Housing and Urban Development.

mobility from 1970 to 1975. Although the Census Bureau does not collect data on cross-jurisdictional moves within counties, Dagger notes that 17.1 percent of the population moved into a different county in this period. Reasoning that "residents of metropolis need not move far to find themselves in a different political unit," Dagger (1981: 726) concluded that 20 percent should be a conservative estimate of the proportion of the population changing residence to a different political jurisdiction in a five-year period.

The Kansas City survey did not include a follow-up item on where individuals were planning to move. If the breakdown from the HUD national sample survey applies to the Kansas City situation, however, we would expect only a little more than half of the movers to be planning cross-jurisdictional moves. This being the case, only about 9 percent of the Kansas City respondents would fall into the category of possible Tiebout-ites.

This discussion of the extent of cross-jurisdictional mobility is significant largely because it identifies the pool of individuals planning moves that might be influenced by finding a better local government tax and service package. Not all cross-jurisdictional moves are made for this reason, however, and existing research on residential relocation does not place a great deal of weight on this factor.

Traditionally, this research distinguishes "migration," which involves relocation across county lines, from intraurban "mobility"—a distinction that unfortunately does not match the relevant distinction here of cross-jurisdictional versus within-same-city moves. Nevertheless, migration would, in virtually all cases, entail a change in local government jurisdiction, whereas mobility only sometimes entails such a change.

Analyses of migration have been dominated by the economic opportunity explanation (Simmons, 1968: 623). That is, job change, not the search for a preferable local government, has been the keystone for understanding the longer-distance moves that are the focus of migration studies. By contrast, John Quigley notes that a "consumption" framework underlies analyses of intraurban mobility: "Short-distance intrametropolitan moves are quite frequently made without changes in the location or the type of job of the wage earner(s) in the household. Thus, the analysis of intrametropolitan mobility behavior generally proceeds by relating the propensity to move of individuals or groups to measures of the expected consumption benefits and costs, considering household income as exogenous" (1980: 42). Unfortunately, devising a satisfactory model of mobility has, according to Quigley, proved "intractable" because little is known about the demand functions for the different items in the consumption basket. Housing characteristics, characteristics of neighbors, access to shopping, and many other considerations as well as the quality of local government services are part of the consumption basket, and the relative importance of each is difficult to determine.

In studies of residential location, according to King and Golledge, "Frequently assessments of *why* people move are made by examining patterns of actual flow and associations between those and social, economic, spatial, and similar variables" (1978: 314). Quigley's point is that such a mode of analysis is unlikely to yield a satisfactory micro model of intraurban residential choice. Nor is this method likely to provide clear-cut evidence of the relative importance of urban government's performance in the residential choice calculus.

Schneider and Logan (1982: 97) observed, however, that tests of the hypothesis that the performance of urban government is important in residential choice will require analysis of survey data. Again, the 1978 HUD national sample survey and the Kansas City survey are useful.

The HUD survey provides several alternative ways of assessing the importance of urban services and taxes in the residential location calculus. For example, all respondents (except those who had lived in the same community all their lives) were asked their reasons for moving to the community in which they currently lived. Specifically, they were asked to rate the importance (very important, important, not too important, and did not affect deci-

Demand-Making and Mobility

sion) of fourteen possible reasons, some of which clearly relate to urban services or taxes and some of which do not. Table 5-2 shows the percentages of respondents answering "very important" or "important" to each of the items.

Housing quality and price are, according to this measure, the most consistently important considerations. Only one of the overtly public service–related items (quality of schools) was important for at least half of the respondents; the other obvious urban service item (mass transit) was important for less than one-fourth of the respondents, and taxes were important for just over one-third. The relevance of public services may, of course, be indirectly reflected in other items, such as those on neighborhood safety and whether the neighborhood was well kept.

TABLE 5-2. *Reasons for Selecting Present Location, 1978 National Sample (percentages)*

Reason	Important or Very Important
Housing in a range I/we could afford	75.2
Housing of the quality, type, or size wanted	70.2
Safe neighborhood	67.6
Neighborhood was well kept	64.1
Location convenient to work	55.5
Good schools	50.6
Taxes reasonable compared to other places	35.2
To be near relatives or friends	33.8
Convenient shopping	32.2
Job change	30.8
Green, open spaces	30.6
Recreation/entertainment/cultural opportunities	24.5
Ethnic/racial backgrounds of people living here	24.2
Good mass transportation	23.8

N's range from 5,927 to 5,974 depending on the number of missing cases for the particular item.

Source: Quality of Urban Life, a 1978 survey conducted by Louis Harris and Associates for the Department of Housing and Urban Development.

Table 5-2 does not show the relative importance of the various factors to the respondents. To ascertain the relative importance of urban services and tax reasons compared to other reasons, we can consider responses to a follow-up HUD survey item that asked respondents which of the reasons was the most important in their decision to move to the community in which they currently lived. Table 5-3 presents the results, with many of the response categories collapsed because of the small numbers of respondents choosing them.

Table 5-3 makes clear that local government services and taxes are not the most important consideration for residential choice for the overwhelming majority of individuals. They may, as Table 5-2 suggested, be important considerations for citizens, but they do not dominate the choice of location. Rather, urban services and taxes presumably are second-level considerations in what Quigley describes as a complex decision process: "At the most general level, households with given economic and demographic characteristics jointly choose a job, an employment location, a residence, a residential location, and a basket of 'other goods,' subject to a variety of financial, physical, and information constraints" (1980: 40).

The HUD survey provides another means of assessing the importance of local government services (but not taxes) in residential mobility. Unlike the foregoing survey items, which focus on reasons for choosing the community of current residence, this second method focuses on factors that may cause respondents to move from the community in which they reside. Specifically, a battery of items was presented, asking respondents whether they would definitely, probably, probably not, or definitely not consider moving if each of a series of conditions in their community worsened in the next two years. In short, this set of items provides an assessment of which are the more important "push" factors for mobility, whereas the items considered earlier implicitly focus on "pull" factors—the most important factors bringing people to the communities in which they live.

As Table 5-4 shows, public services, from this perspective, are

Demand-Making and Mobility

TABLE 5-3. *Most Important Reason for Selecting Present Location, 1978 National Sample (percentages)*

Reason	Most Important
Convenient work location/job change	27.2
Housing price/quality	22.4
Good mass transportation	19.5
Near relatives or friends/backgrounds of people	9.9
Good schools	5.3
Safe neighborhood	4.6
Open spaces/shopping/recreation/cultural	5.0
Neighborhood well kept	1.2
Taxes	0.8
No most important reason	4.1
Total	100.0
(N)	(6,984)

Source: Quality of Urban Life, a 1978 survey conducted by Louis Harris and Associates for the Department of Housing and Urban Development.

at least as important as any other item on the list. No one of these items stands out as being a "push" factor for the majority of respondents, and only one—leisure time activities—appears to be a less prevalent "push" factor than the others. In contrast with analyses above, however, which show public services to be of secondary importance at best in the choice of a place to live, these data suggest that declining quality of public services constitutes a relatively important reason for exiting from the place where one lives.

This last set of HUD survey items presents hypothetical situations of worsening conditions and asks if respondents would move. In the Kansas City survey, the importance of public services in the decision to move was assessed in a non-hypothetical way. That is, all those who indicated that they definitely or probably would move in the next couple of years were asked: How important, if at all, is the quality of government and its services in your thinking about moving? The results suggest that

TABLE 5-4. *The Decision to Move under Various Hypothetical Circumstances (percentages)*

If Listed Item Gets Worse in Next Two Years	Would Definitely or Probably Move
Public services provided in this city—garbage collection, street conditions, fire and police protection, public transport	35.1
Natural environment of this city—the quality of air and water, amount of noise	34.6
Physical characteristics of this city—condition of the streets, buildings, and housing, availability of parks, and the degree of crowding and congestion	32.2
Job opportunities available in this city for people like yourself	31.0
Public schools in this city	29.3
Social environment in this city—people who live here and their attitudes toward you	28.7
Leisure time facilities, available in this city—parks, playgrounds, restaurants, movies, plays, and museums	18.6

Source: Quality of Urban Life, a 1978 survey conducted by Louis Harris and Associates for the Department of Housing and Urban Development.

the hypothetical items on the HUD survey by no means overstate the importance of public services. Nearly one-third (30.3 percent) of those planning to move said that government and its services constituted a "very" important consideration in their plans; another 28.6 percent indicated that government services were "somewhat" important, and 41 percent said that government services were "not at all" important.

In sum, this tour through existing mobility literature with side stops to examine data from both a national sample survey and the Kansas City survey suggests (1) that Americans are mobile, even within a relatively short time frame (five years or less), but that only about half of all moves are likely to be cross-jurisdictional; and (2) that although not all cross-jurisdictional moves necessarily fit the Tiebout model, more than one-third of all national sample respondents said they probably or definitely would move if public services worsened, and nearly one-third of the Kansas City respondents who were planning to move indicated that the quality of public services was a very important factor in their decision to move. Thus, without necessarily adopting the equilibrium model offered by Tiebout, it is reasonable to suggest that his assumption of a link between citizens' evaluations of public services and mobility should be taken seriously. Survey evidence indicates that the quality of local government service is relatively important in the relocation calculus, perhaps not so much in the decision about where to move as in the decision to move.

Admittedly, exit through residential relocation, especially for reasons of discontent with public services, is relatively uncommon. Even so, the survey data for Kansas City show that 8 percent definitely planned to move, and 30 percent of these said that the quality of public services was a very important consideration in their decision. This suggests that over a two-year period the city could lose as much as 2.4 percent of its population for reasons other than the economic opportunity or family cycle and housing market considerations that are difficult for the city to control. Presumably, some portion of this 2.4 percent loss could be retained if public services were more satisfactory.

In fact, Kansas City lost 11.7 percent of its population from 1970 to 1980 (down to 448,159 from 507,330). Such major losses generate considerable consternation among government officials and civic leaders. The usual reaction is to stress the need for economic development to sustain or expand the community's employment base. As important as this may be, the data here suggest that a noteworthy portion of such population decline can be traced to discretionary moves based on quality of life considerations such as public services rather than the necessity of pursuing job opportunities elsewhere.

Political Participation versus Exit

The foregoing section established evidence of a link between citizens' evaluations of the quality of government services and their mobility. Stated another way, there is empirical support for the assumption that family mobility is, at least in part, a function of the level, appropriateness, or quality of services offered by local government. Evidence on the importance of taxes in the relocation calculus is more elusive. The previous section also illustrates that the public service evaluation–mobility link must be treated in proper perspective. Relatively few citizens move solely because of dissatisfaction with public services. Even small losses over time can erode a city's resources; and, as Peterson (1981) rightly emphasizes, loss of population, especially more productive segments of the population, is taken seriously by city leaders.

But do discontented citizens simply move, or do they first engage in acts of political participation intended to ameliorate unsatisfactory conditions? This is the central issue posed by Hirschman (1970). This section considers the relationship between mobility as a response to unsatisfactory local government services (or exit) and various forms of political participation (or voice), including citizen-initiated contacting of government officials.

Hirschman offers two hypotheses in this regard. The first hypothesis, that exit diminishes voice, can be interpreted in three somewhat different ways. At one level, it may mean that those who move repeatedly never develop the community attachment or sense of stake that are prerequisites for active involvement in public affairs. This point of view is adopted by Dagger, for example, who argues that there are "unsettling effects of such widespread mobility on citizenship. Some of the obstacles to political participation, such as the legal barrier of voter registration and the sheer lack of familiarity with political issues and personalities in the new location, are apparent. . . . Citizenship grows out of attachment to a place and its people—out of a sense of community—which only forms over time. When we move about frequently, we find it all but impossible to acquire this attachment" (1981: 727). Research on the link between length of residence in a community and political participation supports this viewpoint on the dampening effect of mobility on participation (Alford and Lee, 1968; Bollens and Schmandt, 1970).

Two other interpretations of the "exit diminishes voice" hypothesis are more salient in Hirschman's analysis and more relevant from the perspective of the community that is facing a potential loss of valued members. Exit can be said to diminish voice in the sense that the very existence of this escape alternative discourages citizens from the potentially longer-term and more uncertain route of pressing for improvements in the city that is disappointing them. In other words, exit is an easier and surer response; hence discontented citizens are likely to take the exit option without bothering to "voice" (Hirschman, 1970: 43). As evidence for this hypothesis, we would expect to find that those planning to move are notably less likely than other citizens to have engaged in various forms of political participation.

Yet another interpretation offered by Hirschman is that exit diminishes voice in the sense that the most politically active members of the community, by taking the exit option, leave behind a citizenry less predisposed to political action. In short, exit can diminish voice by creating a "situation which paralyzes voice by depriving it of its principal agents" (Hirschman, 1970: 51). As evidence for this interpretation, we would expect to find that those planning to move show a higher propensity for political participation than others in the community.

Finally, Hirschman (1970: 37) offers the hypothesis that exit is an "option of last resort" after voice has been tried without success. This hypothesis and the interpretation that exit diminishes voice by robbing it of its principal agents are not mutually exclusive. The "exit as an option of last resort" hypothesis also presumes that exiters are among the most politically active members of the community. To support this hypothesis it would be necessary to show that exiters have been frustrated in attempts to solve problems through political participation.

Table 5-5 presents data from the Kansas City citizen survey relevant to these issues. The first column in the table shows the participation levels of nonmovers—those who said they were definitely or probably not going to move in the next year or two. The second and third columns show the rates for movers for whom the quality of government and its services was very important in the moving decision (the "Tiebout-ites") and those for whom this factor was not at all important. In addition to citizen-initiated contacting, the table includes four other participation items—voting in the last local election, attending political meetings (such as fund-raisers, rallies, or meetings with candidates) in the last three or four years, membership in any "group or organization in the community that works to solve community problems," and working with neighbors to help solve a local problem. The former two items are examples of electoral participation; the latter two of what Verba and Nie (1972) call "communal" participation.

The table shows no evidence that exit diminishes voice in its electoral or communal participation forms; there is evidence, however, that exit diminishes demand-making in the form of citizen-initiated contacting of local officials. On the former count, we see that Tiebout-ites have been neither more nor less electorally and communally active in the community than either of the other groups. Hence we must reject the notion that Tiebout-ites choose the exit option with minimal prior voice. Similarly, there is no evidence that the departure of these Tiebout-ites leaves behind a citizenry less disposed to electoral or communal involvement, for there are no significant differences in electoral and communal participation levels between movers and nonmovers.

Citizen-initiated contacting of government officials is another matter entirely. Table 5-5 indicates that exit does diminish this

TABLE 5-5. *Mobility and Political Participation (percentages)*

	Nonmovers	Intended Movers, for Whom Government Services Are Very Important ("Tiebout-ites")	Not at All Important (Other Movers)
Voted in last election	62	56	50
Attended a political meeting in last 3–4 years	20	25	23
Worked with neighbors on local problem (ever)	39	38	36
Membership in community organization	21	25	17
Contacted local official in past year	27*	49*	31*

*In difference of proportions tests, the differences between Tiebout-ites and each of the other groups with respect to contacting are significant at $< .01$ level. None of the other differences in proportions represented in the table are significant at the .05 level.

N's, depending upon the number of missing cases for various items, range from 1,674 to 1,717 nonmovers, from 102 to 104 "Tiebout-ites," and from 139 to 141 other movers. Intended movers who said government and its services were "somewhat" important in their moving plans are excluded from the table.

form of demand-making, in the sense that the Tiebout-ites are the most contacting-prone group, so their departure would rob the community of its most vocal constituency. In short, there is evidence for Hirschman's notion that exit dampens voice by robbing it of its principal agents, but only with respect to voice in the form of citizen-initiated contacting of government officials.

By the same token, the unusually high level of contacting propensity on the part of Tiebout-ites suggests that exit is, in many cases, an option of last resort after voice has been tried and has failed. As noted above, however, this hypothesis would be still better supported if there were evidence that Tiebout-ites not only have engaged in demand-making before choosing mobility, but also that they have been disappointed in their demand-making efforts. Table 5-6 provides supporting evidence with respect to citizens' evaluations of how the city handled their contacts.

TABLE 5-6. *Mobility and Evaluations of Government's Response to Contact (percentages)*

"Poor" or "Unacceptable" Rating on	Nonmovers	Tiebout-ites	Other Movers
Promptness of handling contact	30*	47*	37
Effectiveness of handling contact	31†	49†	33
Courtesy of handling contact	6‡	16‡	14

*,†,‡Indicate pairs for which a difference of proportions test is significant at < .01 level.

N's, depending upon missing cases for various items, are between 434 and 443 nonmovers, 51 Tiebout-ites, and 42 or 43 other movers.

Although the Tiebout-ites have been more prone to voice complaints and demands, Table 5-6 shows that they are more likely than the nonmovers to have been dissatisfied with the results of the process. They are particularly disgruntled with government's promptness and effectiveness in handling the matter about which they made contact. Whereas fewer than one-third of the nonmovers and a little more than a third of the other movers were dissatisfied with government's promptness, nearly one-half of the Tiebout-ites were dissatisfied; and although about one-third of the nonmovers and the other movers were dissatisfied with government officials' handling of their problems, about half of the Tiebout-ites were dissatisfied.

There is also more general evidence that, for the Tiebout-ites, the decision to move occurs in a context of frustration with the

Demand-Making and Mobility 159

results of voice. Although the citizen survey did not ask citizens directly to evaluate the results of such forms of political participation as electoral involvement or neighborhood organization activity, it contained two measures of citizens' overall assessment of local government's responsiveness. As shown in Chapter 4, these perceptions of government's responsiveness were linked with citizens' evaluations of their contacting experience; here, these perceptions are treated as reflections of the citizens' summative evaluation of their experiences with political participation.

Table 5-7 shows that, just as in the narrower evaluation of government's responses to individual contacts, citizens' evaluations of the overall responsiveness of government are not distributed evenly across the mobility categories. Movers, especially the Tiebout-ites, were more likely than nonmovers to be critical of local government's responsiveness. In short, Table 5-7 shows, for the full set of respondents, what Table 5-6 showed for the subset who had recently contacted a city official about a problem—that Tiebout-ites exit after voice has, from their perspective, failed.

TABLE 5-7. *Mobility and Perceptions of Government Responsiveness (percentages)*

	Nonmovers	Tiebout-ites	Other Movers
Government officials are "only slightly" or "not at all" responsive to my concerns	27*	37*	34
Kansas City government does not try to provide the kind of services people in my neighborhood want	11†	26†	15

*or†Indicates pairs for which a difference of proportions test is significant at < .01 level.

N's, depending upon missing cases for the items, are 1,338 and 1,528 nonmovers, 91 or 97 Tiebout-ites, and 106 or 124 other movers.

Discussion

For the citizen who approaches city hall with a complaint or a request about a problem, there are immediate consequences if the city does not respond adequately. A malfunctioning street light is not fixed, a dangerous intersection is left unattended, a pothole remains unfilled, the citizen continues to fear that the neighborhood's level of police protection is inadequate, or some other problem is unresolved. As we have seen in Chapter 4, there are second-order consequences for the citizen as well. Unsatisfactory experiences in these direct citizen–city hall interactions can erode the citizen's confidence in local government's capacity or willingness to respond.

In this chapter, we find that there are third-order consequences as well, which have important implications for the city. Dissatisfaction with the quality of local government services can be an important "push" factor in the residential relocation calculus and hence a contributor to urban decline.

This conclusion may not surprise those for whom the Tiebout metaphor of "voting with one's feet" is intuitively obvious. The importance of the link between government services and family mobility is often overlooked, however, in part because studies of migration have been more numerous than studies of intraurban mobility, and the economic factors that loom large in the former easily dominate thinking about residential relocation generally.

If, as Peterson (1981) argues, cities are concerned about the potential loss of productive, taxpaying citizens, at least two preventive strategies are possible. The first is a proactive strategy, in which city decision makers are "responsive in advance" to the concerns of the productive segments of the community. As Peterson (1981) argues, this strategy is essentially an emphasis on developmental expenditures, combined with appropriate levels of basic housekeeping services and with redistributive programs held to a minimum. The implicit assumption is that the maintenance of an economically viable community is the main interest of productive, potentially mobile segments of the community;

there is less attention to the possibility that the quality of basic housekeeping services can be significant in citizens' relocation calculus.

City decision makers may also use a reactive strategy, in which responsiveness to individual complaints and requests for service is a key method for sustaining the confidence of citizen-consumers. This approach is exemplified in the adoption of centralized complaint units in many cities, and it reflects Hirschman's (1970) notion that cities, like firms, need critical feedback to remain viable. Policies that enhance the economic competitiveness of the community are not, from this perspective, necessarily enough to keep the loyalty of productive citizens. Responsiveness to their concerns about everyday city service issues is also critical.

The reactive strategy requires that potentially mobile citizens register their discontent before choosing the exit option. The analysis here shows that, at least in Kansas City, exit is chosen as an option of last resort after voice. If anything, those who moved were more "voice active" than those they left behind, although they were also more disappointed with the results of their demand-making. This suggests that the city at a minimum has the opportunity to respond to demands in such a way as to head off exit. It also suggests that, if the response is not satisfactory, the community ultimately loses through exit some of its principal demand-making agents—a result that Hirschman (1970) argues is detrimental to the long-run viability of the community.

6

Urban Governance and Demand Overload

☑ ☑ ☑
☑ ☑ ☑

Throughout this book, citizen-initiated contacts with urban officials have been treated as constituting a significant form of political demand-making in the urban setting. Citizen-initiated contacting is an important form of demand-making in part because it involves more direct, personal demands than those that can be registered through voting or interest-group activity; it is also significant in that urban service delivery systems are frequently geared to respond to such demands, hence, the distribution of such services is linked to patterns of citizen-initiated contacting. Finally, this form of direct citizen demand-making is significant for the onus it places on urban government to respond to the demands.

But is citizen-initiated contacting simply a manifestation of demand-making that is of special interest for urban scholars or does it reflect broader trends toward heightened citizen expectations of government and increasing demands on government at all levels? This chapter pursues the latter possibility, arguing that urban government is subject to the same escalation in demands that many analysts claim is causing a stalemate of national-level governance in the postindustrial era. The causes and implications of demand overload are explored and applied to the specific case of demands for service delivery in the urban context. In short, the chapter sets the citizen-initiated contacting phenomenon in a much broader perspective of demand escalation in postindustrial society.

Government in a High-Demand Age

There is a considerable body of scholarship arguing that, in the United States specifically and in postindustrial societies generally, governments are overloaded with demands—demands that ask far more than was expected of government in the past. Daniel Bell's (1975) discussion of a "revolution of rising entitlements" is perhaps the best exemplar of this viewpoint, which has also been advanced by Samuel Huntington (1975) and others (e.g., Daniel Patrick Moynihan and Irving Kristol) in what Roger Benjamin (1980) calls the "overload" school. From this perspective, an ideology of postindustrial society is the encouragement of political participation and demand-making, and the many competing demands upon government that result have led to a "crisis of governance" (Benjamin, 1980: 102).

Helen Ingram and Dean Mann likewise point to "excessive policy demand" as a current problem of government, especially insofar as high expectations of government imply a greater likelihood of failure: "Ills we once accepted as inevitable are now expected to be assuaged by government. An old adage dictates, 'Expect nothing, avoid disappointment.' If the corollary of the principle holds, 'Expect everything, guarantee disappointment,' the mounting demands placed upon modern government predetermine perceptions of failure" (1980: 17). The "overload" school's arguments are echoed in Yair Aharoni's thesis that the governments of developed nations throughout the world now are expected to create a "no-risk society": "A new social order has evolved that started with a reliance by citizens on government for the solution to certain economic, social, and cultural problems and has grown to include pressures on government to mitigate almost every risk any individual might be asked to bear" (1981: 1).

In short, there is a growing consensus that governments in postindustrial societies face heavy demands for solutions to all manner of problems that were not necessarily laid at their doorsteps in the past; further, the citizens' heightened expectations that supposedly fuel these demands will, if anything, generate an ongoing escalation of demands, to the point at which governments are stalemated from acting on competing demands or at which disappointment with government's solutions modifies expectations downward.

Although the arguments of the "overload" school are pervasive and in many ways compelling, they may appear to clash with empirical research on public opinion and political mobilization. Paul Sniderman and Richard Brody (1977), for example, argue that in the United States, an "ethic of self-reliance" militates against politicization of personal problems. Even when "socially located" problems (those whose locus of concern is society rather than the self) are distinguished from "self-located" problems, Brody and Sniderman (1977) found that citizens with socially located problems are not especially politically activated (at least in the sense of voting). Furthermore, when respondents were asked who ought to be helping with their problem, Brody and Sniderman (1977: 351) found that nearly two-thirds of the respondents were self-reliant (that is, they believed they should handle their own problem or rely on some other private individual, usually family) and that only one-third were "government reliant."

Similarly, Kay Schlozman and Sidney Verba (1979), noting that the unemployed in America have been surprisingly quiescent, provide a thorough analysis of the reasons for this lack of political mobilization. Their conclusion, as in Brody and Sniderman's analysis of the ethic of self-reliance, is that the prevailing social ideology in this country militates against the politicization of even this most severe of personal economic problems: "Beliefs about social reality—about either opportunities for advancement or the class structure—seem relatively impermeable to the effects of personal experience . . . it seems that the prospects for political mobilization are relatively limited. Americans' views are characterized by an individualistic belief in opportunity and a low level of class consciousness, and furthermore, there seems to be no link between personal experience and more abstract understanding of society" (Schlozman and Verba, 1979: 155–56). These research results are a far cry from the portrait of American society painted by adherents of the "overload" school; nor does that school of thought seem to mesh particularly well with recent analyses of the strength of self-help and voluntary action movements (Boyte, 1980).

Yet, different as they seem, both the overload school's analysis and arguments that an ethic of individualistic self-reliance underlies American politics can be correct. That is, heightened expectations and demands upon government can coexist with belief in individualism and self-reliance. Charles Elder and Roger Cobb (1983: 100–101), for example, argue that "without displacing the standing prescription of limited government" or the "premium placed on individual achievement and freedom," the New Deal introduced to the American political culture the conception that government was responsible for individual welfare. The "duality" in American political culture that results does involve values in tension, but such tensions, apparent inconsistencies, or complexities within value systems have often been noted by scholars of American public opinion (Converse, 1964; Sniderman, Brody, and Kuklinski, 1984). In short, without rejecting the claim that individualism and self-reliance are strong orienting principles in American politics, we can also take seriously those observers who claim that the American public expects much more from government than ever before.

The overload school typically emphasizes that demands on national governments have escalated. Is this perspective also relevant for urban governments? Some would argue that the demand overload school of thought is not the most useful for understanding the pressures facing urban governments today. Rather, it might be argued that the difficulties cities face result from limitations in their capacity. Specifically, cities face a crunch because of limitations on the revenue side, rather than escalations on the demand side. Erosion of the tax base and other limitations on revenue-raising capacity, coupled with rising costs of providing a given level of services, are more important factors from this point of view.

Clearly, revenue is relevant to the considerations at issue here. If there were no constraints on revenue, escalating demands would not overload government, either fiscally or politically; and clearly, some urban governments do face problems arising from factors as diverse as erosion of the tax base, state limitations on taxing ability, and political limits to revenue-raising.

There are, however, good reasons for emphasizing the demand side of the equation at least as much as the revenue side. For one thing, city government revenues have been expanding until very recently. Between 1972 and 1977, total municipal government revenues rose 74.4 percent and between 1977 and 1982, revenues rose 57.2 percent (U.S. Bureau of the Census, 1982). Clark and Ferguson (1983: 86) show that every form of local government revenue has grown steadily from 1959 to 1980. When the effects of inflation are considered, the revenue picture is not as healthy. In constant (1967) dollars, total municipal revenue increased 20 percent between 1972 and 1977 and fell off 1 percent from the 1977 level by 1982. Clark and Ferguson note, however, that "inflation and recession are fiscally troublesome, but cities generally suffer less than private firms and the federal government" (1983: 90).

There is other evidence that, despite (or perhaps because of) New York City's fiscal scare in the mid-1970s, municipal governments generally are in reasonably good fiscal health. In a study of thirty-eight of the nation's largest cities, for example, Pearl Kamer (1983: 76–77) reports that general revenues (in constant 1972 dollars) in the cities with declining populations grew from $339 per capita in 1969 to $427 per capita in 1975 and $449 per capita in 1979. In the growing and "mixed" population change cities, growth in revenue over this period was more dramatic. Roy Bahl (1984: 40) reports that although the operating surplus of state and local governments has fluctuated between 1970 and 1981, it has not been less than $8.8 billion (in current dollars) in the period and was at $19.5 billion in 1981. Furthermore, Bahl (1984: 45) notes that, contrary to common wisdom, these state-local government surpluses are not concentrated at the state level.

All of this is not to claim that the fiscal situation is rosy for all urban governments, or that it is improving in the mid-1980s. In part, the reasonable fiscal health of most large cities since 1975 has been the result of large increases in federal aid; but a slowdown in this source has begun and is likely to continue (Bahl, 1984: 69). Furthermore, aggregate data on urban finances tend to mask real variability in cities' fiscal health; and the validity of single measures (such as operating surplus) as indicators of fiscal health has been challenged. For these reasons, considerable effort has been devoted in recent years to the conceptualization and measurement of fiscal stress in cities (Nathan and Adams, 1976; Stanley, 1980; Burchell and Listokin, 1981; Clark and Ferguson, 1983; Kamer, 1983).

These studies of fiscal stress, however, bring us back to the main point at issue—the importance of the escalation of demand. Research on fiscal stress suggests that factors on the demand side are at least as crucial as those on the revenue side. Irene Rubin (1982), for example, suggests that the many analyses of fiscal stress provide three types of explanations: a migration and tax base erosion model, a bureaucratic growth model, and a political vulnerability model (see also Kamer, 1983: 3–4). In the migration and tax base erosion model, population shifts are said to have created greater demands for expenditures, especially for social services, in the very cities that are losing the tax base to sustain such growth in expenditures. The political vulnerability model suggests that in some cities the demands of various interest groups force political leaders to overspend relative to the city's fiscal capacity, thus yielding fiscal stress. Only the bureaucratic growth model largely neglects the role of escalating demands from the public. It posits instead that ever-expanding budgets are a function of the self-interests and incentives of the permanent bureaucracy. Even this model can, as we will see below, also tie indirectly to considerations of escalation of demand from the public. For the moment, however, it is important to note that demand pressures are critical components of two of these three explanatory models of fiscal stress.

In sum, the overload school of thought, with its emphasis on the escalation of demand, is likely to be very relevant to our understanding of urban governance and fiscal stress. Clearly, escalation of demand is problematic only within the context of the city's limited fiscal capacity. But even in cities that are not exemplars of the long-term problem of erosion of the tax base facing many northeastern cities, escalating demands can result in an overload, as some rapidly growing sunbelt communities have discovered.

One other caveat about application of the overload perspective to the urban scene is in order. Demand overload has been most readily conceptualized as involving some version of "hyperpluralism"—an overload of demands emanating from multiple and conflicting interest groups. This perspective has readily been applied to the urban context, as in Yates's (1977) metaphor of "street fighting pluralism," which he uses to describe the "political free-for-all" that results when fragmented local government authority faces heavy demands from many different groups.

As significant as these group-based demands are, cities also face an influx of individual demands for services via the phenomenon of citizen-initiated contacting. In Kansas City, the 45,000 or so complaints and requests that the Action Center receives each year are, as we have seen, only the tip of the iceberg. Many more citizens contact service delivery departments directly. At least one contact with a local official in the past year was reported by 28 percent of all respondents. If that figure is used as a point estimate for the population of Kansas City, it translates into a conservative estimate of more than 142,000 contacts annually. Many of these are relatively simple requests; others have more significant implications involving the city's resources. All however, are demands for government attention to some problem.

When adherents of the overload school speak of increasing demands upon national governments, they typically focus on conflicting interest groups and the pressures they exert for new government programs and protections. Whether the demands of these interest groups are accurate reflections of mass public expectations of government is an open question.

Urban governments likewise face multiple interest groups and pressures to take on new problems and responsibilities. Citizen-initiated contacting in the urban context, however, is a special form of demand-making. Although it is affected by organized groups in the city (see, for example, Chapter 3 on the role of neighborhood associations in the contacting process), citizen-initiated contacting is also a highly individualized activity. It is, therefore, perhaps a more useful barometer of the mass public's expectations of government than are interest-group activities. In addition, citizen-initiated contacting does not typically involve demands for new urban government programs. As Jones indicates, "Most contacts initiated by citizens and directed at local government are requests for services that are already being delivered by established, ongoing government agencies. They are not demands for broad policy initiatives, new directions by government, nor for the establishment of new governmental organizations" (1980: 6). In short, the overload school's diagnosis of escalating demands is applicable to the urban context, but with special care. Much of the demand-making that is directed at urban government is not interest-group pressure for new programs and policies but pressure from individuals for existing urban bureaucracies to deliver services.

If urban governments, like national governments, are facing rising expectations and demand overload in postindustrial society, what are the reasons? The following section explores various explanations for this escalation, which were largely developed to account for the "revolution of rising entitlements" at the national level. The explanations are also relevant to the urban situation although, as we shall see, additional perspectives unique to the urban context are important.

Accounting for the Escalation of Demand

In this section, we consider four distinctive (albeit not mutually exclusive) explanations for citizens' heightened expectations and increasing demands upon government. Three of these explanations are variants of the "public sector creates its own demand" perspective; the fourth is derived from the urban political economy literature on the fiscal crisis of the state.

As Aaron Wildavsky (1979), H. Brinton Milward (1980), Michael Lipsky (1980), and others have noted, the demand overload that governments face is, ironically, often of government's own making. There are three different senses in which government can be said to create its own demand. First there is the argument that public-sector officials, especially bureaucrats, find it in their self-interest to create pressure for new programs, expanded policy initiatives, and increased budgets (Niskanen, 1971; Milward, 1980). This version of the "public sector creates its own demand" argument is essentially an elaboration on the theme of bureaucratic empire-building or an entrepreneurialism argument. It stresses the importance of bureaucratic-professional expertise in policy formulation and the manner in which private-sector providers, interest groups, and ambitious bureaucrats combine to form "policy communities" that generate expanded government activity.

Second, it is possible for government to create its own demand in the sense that government's attempts to solve a given set of problems generate a host of additional problems. This happens because public policies frequently have unintended consequences and because public policies devoted to one problem interact in unforeseen ways with other public policies. Perhaps the chief proponent of this policy complexity interpretation is Aaron Wildavsky, who argues: "Again we see that policy problems rarely appear to be solved because past solutions create future problems faster than present troubles can be left behind. When policy spaces were lightly filled, programs could be pursued on their own merits . . . today, however, policy spaces are dense; any major move sets off series of changes, many of which —because they are large and connected—inevitably transform any problem they were originally supposed to solve" (1979: 70–71).

Both the entrepreneurialism and the policy complexity arguments are useful explanations of some aspects of demand overload in the urban context. Much of the expanded activity of urban government with respect to tackling problems of poverty and urban decay in the late 1960s and 1970s fits the entrepreneurialism interpretation, with its emphasis on bureaucrats, intellectuals, interest groups, and professional associations functioning in proactive "policy communities" that encompass both local and federal officials. The policy complexity argument nicely captures the dilemma of many city governments that institute policies to attract new industry, only to face a host of transportation, flood control, or other infrastructure problems associated with industrial development and to discover that solutions to some of these problems may bump up against existing policies respecting environmental protection, housing, and the like.

Neither the entrepreneurialism nor the policy complexity argument is particularly useful in accounting for escalating demand in the form of direct, citizen-initiated requests for public services. As noted above, this form of demand-making does not normally involve pressures for new policy initiatives or new government programs, nor is the demand typically expressed by interest groups functioning within "policy communities." Hence the entrepreneurialism interpretation is not particularly applicable.

Citizen-initiated contacting typically involves demands that some existing urban service bureaucracy provide a solution to one of the basic "housekeeping" problems for which the bureau is ostensibly responsible. Such demands can escalate in the sense that the bureaucracy is being asked to deliver higher-quality or more frequent service than before, in the sense that less severely problematic conditions are being called to the attention of the bureaucracy, or simply in that greater numbers of individuals are calling problems to the attention of these urban service bureaucracies. These basic urban services are not, by and large, directed at complex social problems about which causal knowledge is incomplete, nor are they exemplars of the "large solutions" that Wildavsky (1979) argues are likely to have multiple, unintended consequences and to cause still further problems as one solution bumps into another. Hence the policy complexity argument is not a particularly useful interpretation of escalating demands for basic urban services, although we might envision a useful variant of it. Urban bureaucracies do make errors, and some urban service delivery agents are incompetent or lax in the performance of their duties. Mishandling of requests for delivery of services often generates a stream of complaints and follow-up demands from the citizenry; and if the mismanagement of the original problem is bad enough, second-order problems requiring greater government effort can be created. In this "mismanagement" sense, Wildavsky's argument that government action can create additional problems for government does apply to the case at hand.

There is, however, a third interpretation of the way in which government can "create its own demand," which is especially relevant for understanding growth even in the most particularistic of citizen demands for basic urban services. This interpretation emphasizes the manner in which government can, either intentionally or inadvertently, contribute to escalating expectations from citizens. It has been argued, for example, that the rhetoric of the urban reform movement convinced urban residents that they have a right to high-quality urban services and that the growth of centralized complaints units contributes further to this entitlement mentality (Sharp, 1984c). In a related vein, Lipsky argues that even the most straightforward efforts toward responsiveness are part of the demand-creation process: "[Demand] not only requires a demander but also a more or less encouraging supplier. It is meaningless to specify a level of demand unless this is accompanied by a positive (if implicit) degree of receptivity. . . . Demand as an expression of desire for services is a meaningful concept only if it is accompanied by explication of the extent to which demand was sought out" (1980: 34–35). In short, the more that local governments attempt to provide basic services in a neutral, professionally competent manner and to provide institutional arrangements to maximize the accountability of urban service bureaucracies to citizen-consumers, the more citizens will be inclined to turn to government for solutions to problems in their neighborhood.

In a larger sense, this interpretation of government creating its own demand by enhancing citizens' expectations is consistent with analyses of the growth of "consumerism" in postindustrial society. Brittan, for example, argues: "Consumerism also involves a psychology of insatiability. Once the broad masses of the population have been exposed to the benefits of mass production they develop a taste for consumer goods which is incapable of satisfaction . . . in other words, there seems to be a peculiar reversal of the 'law of diminishing returns'; instead, the 'law of increasing returns' seems to hold—the more one has, the more one wants" (1977: 63). Translating to the case of local public services, this consumerism perspective would state that the more the broad mass of the population is exposed to the problem-solving capacities of urban government's service-delivery bureaucracies, the more they develop a taste for these services which is incapable of satisfaction.

Analysts of consumer society have not typically drawn this analogy between consumerism with respect to private goods and consumerism with respect to public services. Instead, consumption of private goods has been treated as a "privatizing" phenomenon that alienates individuals from the public sphere (Brittan, 1977). Hirschman (1982) also sees private consumption and involvement in public affairs as separate lifestyle orientations, but he takes the analysis one step further. According to Hirschman, disappointment with the former leads individuals to embrace the latter: "The turn to the public life would not come about as a direct result of disappointment over any specific consumption experience. Rather, these experiences are responsible for the deflation of an ideology that had presided over the quest for private happiness. To the extent that this ideology is resolutely 'antipublic,' its collapse is likely to lead to a search for meaningful participation in public affairs" (1982: 67).

The argument here, however, is that escalating demands for public services go hand in hand with consumerism in the private sphere. High expectations with respect to urban services, in other words, are part and parcel of a broader consumption orientation that prevails in a society dominated by a "service economy" (Fuchs, 1968).

There is a way in which this argument can be squared with the viewpoint represented by Hirschman and Brittan. That is, demand-making with respect to public services can be defined as something less than "meaningful participation in public affairs." The individual who calls city hall to complain about street repairs, to request more frequent police patrol in the neighborhood, or to demand that something be done about storm sewer flooding may not, from this perspective, be having a meaningful public participation experience. For the citizen, the experience may be essentially the same as returning a defective piece of merchandise to the local department store.

There is surely some truth to this perspective. When citizens make direct demands on city government for attention to problems with urban service delivery, they typically enter into a relatively straightforward, limited-involvement activity, albeit one that can take a substantial amount of initiative. There need not be a sense of community involvement, there is little to suggest to the citizen that his or her demand may have larger ramifications for the polity, and the interaction with public officials may be so attenuated as to obviate any of the civic learning that is said to accrue from other forms of political participation. In short, it is possible for the individual contactor to experience primarily the "consumer" rather than the "citizenship" role.

By the same token, this contrast between direct citizen demand-making for urban services and other forms of political participation should not be drawn too starkly. As we have seen, the majority of citizens who have made a contact of this kind characterize their action as being geared toward a neighborhood problem, not simply a narrow matter of concern only to themselves or their family. And we have seen that, even though actual contact may be initiated by individuals, neighborhood organizations often play an important role in mobilizing residents to engage in this behavior because it has ramifications for the neighborhood. In short, communal or "public-interest" concerns are often hidden behind the ostensibly individualistic nature of contacting.

The main point, however, is that citizens may have increased expectations of urban government because government's adoption of both a service delivery role and responsibility for maximizing citizen satisfaction legitimize the consumer role for citizens (Sharp, 1980b). The consumer role is familiar in any case because of the transformation of capitalist society from "an economy of production to an economy of mass consumption" (Brittan, 1977: 62). Trends in urban government, ranging from the reform movement's emphasis on neutral competence and professionalization to the institution of complaints units, simply make it easier for citizens to adopt a consumer role with respect to government that parallels their consumer role in the private sector.

So far I have argued that, if there is demand overload facing urban government, it is in part of government's own making. With respect to citizens' direct demands for urban services, entrepreneurialism on the part of bureaucratic officials and the spiraling need for further public programs to correct the problems of previous policies are not the most relevant interpretations of how government can create its own demand. Rather, there is a more subtle dynamic, whereby urban government's adoption of responsibility for basic housekeeping services and its efforts to maximize responsiveness on demand feed citizens' expectations. And, like all forms of consumerism, there can be an element of insatiability to citizens' expectations for public services.

There is yet another interpretation of the demand overload facing urban government—one that has little to do with citizens' expectations. This is the argument, advanced by adherents of the "urban political economy" tradition, that private sector development requires public sector expenditures. This explanation draws heavily on O'Connor's (1973) argument that the role of the state in capitalist society is to provide "social capital" expenditures that sustain labor productivity and lower the costs of class reproduction plus "social expenses" for programs that maintain social control. In short, public sector activity underwrites the private sector.

From the perspective of "urban political economy," demand overload is not really a function of pressures for new programs or particular complaints and requests for services registered by the mass public or interest groups. Indeed, Rich (1982c: 196) claims that "at the most general level, it is capitalists who control city budgets, not local politicians, voters, or municipal employee unions." Demand overload, which shows up in the form of "fiscal crisis," is seen as a function of the "structural domination of capital." That is, urban governments are compelled to provide social capital and social expenses in response to the developmental decisions that capitalists make. Partly because profits are not "socialized" but these supportive costs of capital accumulation are (O'Connor, 1973) and partly because fragmentation of local governments prevents them from recapturing expenses through tax policy (Kennedy, 1984), local governments ultimately face a fiscal crisis.

Rich goes further to argue that social capital programs are more directly supportive of capital accumulation than are social expenses and that the structure of public finance mirrors these capitalist priorities: "In the United States, most locally sponsored capital improvements are funded by bonded indebtedness rather than direct taxation, and many are administered through politically invisible special service districts. By contrast, operating expenses like police and fire protection, sanitation, and social services are funded by highly visible local taxes, and become objects of intense political conflict among elements of the working class" (1982c: 195). In short, the "urban political economy" approach provides a distinctive perspective on the demand overload issue. Escalating popular demands for basic services are simply the more visible aspect of demand upon urban government, and pressures in this area grow as local government strives to maintain its role of ensuring the conditions for private capital accumulation.

There are strong normative overtones to the contrasting explanations of demand escalation outlined above. The overload school attributes demand escalation to rising citizen expectations and government actions that fuel these expectations. This can readily be taken to mean that the mass public expects too much of government, that many demands are not legitimate, and that efforts to limit government to more "realizable policy expectations" (Ingram and Mann, 1980: 19) should be the order of the day.

By contrast, the urban political economy school sees demand overload as a function of the way capitalists milk the public sector for projects and services that contribute to capital accumulation. Empowerment of working-class and disadvantaged groups in urban areas and exploration of the ways "urban social movements, protest, and disorder" (Fainstein and Fainstein, 1982: 16) can modify the structural bias toward capital accumulation become the order of the day.

For our purposes, it is not necessary to choose between these contrasting explanations of demand overload. Direct demands emanating from the mass public are the primary concern here—hence the phenomenon of escalating expectations as described by the overload school is of more immediate interest than the arguments of the urban political economy school. By the same token, urban political economists usefully remind us that demands from the mass public are not the only, perhaps not even the most onerous, source of demand upon urban governments.

Further, they highlight reasons for the sometimes inordinately conflictual nature of the politics of urban service delivery—the visible character of this type of service allocation compared to infrastructure investments and other social capital expenditures (Rich, 1982c). As was shown in Chapter 3, belief that other neighborhoods are better served is a driving force behind citizens' demands upon government, a dynamic that is understandable in the light of expectations of equality in the delivery of urban services. Coupled with the visibility of such delivery, this is what makes direct, citizen-initiated demand-making a significant managerial and political problem for urban governments.

Consequences of the Escalation of Demand

The previous section treats citizen-initiated demands upon urban government as part of a broader demand overload facing government in postindustrial society. Escalating demands do not, of course, constitute an overload unless they exceed government's capacity to respond. Urban bureaucracies are not highly fragile institutions—they can and do adapt, using various decision rules to allocate services in response to demand. Nevertheless, in the current climate of tax and spending limitations on government at all levels, and in the face of the other demands upon government that the urban political economists highlight, heightened expectations for urban services on the part of the mass public can constitute overload on urban government.

This section explores some of the possible consequences of such overload. The most obvious of these consequences are consumer disappointment and related phenomena such as alienation from government and residential relocation (exit). These consequences were discussed in Chapters 4 and 5, so little more need be said of them here.

Equally significant are the adaptive responses that local governments grope for in the face of demand overload. Essentially, five strategies can be envisioned for overloaded local governments. They can (1) attempt to share responsibility for service delivery through "coproduction"; (2) slough off the responsibility to deliver services through privatization strategies; (3) attempt to market services more efficiently by introducing pricelike mechanisms; (4) attempt to respond to mounting service demands while masking actual levels of government expenditure and debt; and (5) ration services.

Perhaps the simplest of these is the last—governments can essentially limit the effective demand facing them by rationing services. As Lipsky (1980) notes, this rationing need not be a matter of official policy. It can involve, instead, the subtle, informal devices street-level bureaucrats use to cope with unreasonable case loads and mismatches between agency resources and client needs. Devices ranging from long waiting lines to perfunctory service to rude behavior on the part of street-level bureaucrats can reduce overload in two ways: by limiting the number of requests that are effectively serviced and by discouraging citizens from registering demands in the future. Such methods, however, only exacerbate consumer disappointment and hide the distributional consequences of rationing strategies.

More formal, authoritative rationing is also effected by chief administrators and elected officials. Decisions that the city will provide trash collection only once a week, that certain areas of the city should have low priority for snow plowing, or that storm sewer flooding problems in a particular area cannot be remedied within existing budget constraints are examples of such decisions. Such formal, authoritative rationing is preferable from the perspective of the democratic theorist because it makes such judgments more visible and subject to public debate. For these very reasons, however, more and more rationing decisions are not made in this formal, visible fashion; instead, they are buried in unpublicized "bureaucratic decision rules" or the informal coping strategies devised by the lowest-level bureaucrats in service delivery agencies.

Perhaps the most popular strategies for dealing with demand overload, at least judging from the current public administration literature, are those that involve the sloughing off of responsibility for service delivery or the introduction of pricelike devices such as user fees—both aspects of privatization of service delivery. Advocates of the former argue that local government should not be a monopoly supplier of all the services that it traditionally has provided. By contracting with or setting up franchising arrangements with private firms, introducing voucher systems, or simply shedding service responsibilities that private firms can conceivably handle, proponents of privatization argue that more efficient and responsive service delivery can be established (Savas, 1982). User fees are also popular because, although service delivery remains the responsibility of government, a pricelike arrangement regulates who gets what, when, and how much. Government thus adopts the values of the market.

These strategies for dealing with overload can be effective, and they should be considered by local government managers. Evidence on actual efficiency gains and service delivery quality under these alternative arrangements is still accumulating, however, and their appropriateness may be contingent upon a variety of local circumstances.

Perhaps more important is consideration of the normative consequences of government's adoption of these privatizing strategies, specifically with regard to impacts on the role of the citizen. As Charles Levine argues, in this model "citizens are consumers, buying privatized services just as they would buy any other service provided by the private sector. . . . This attitude is wholly consistent with the view of the privatizers that the citizen ought to be a consumer, a voter, and perhaps a member of interest groups, nothing more. Public spirited action has no place in this scheme" (1984: 180). Viewed in this light, privatizing strategies constitute an indirect endorsement of consumer-oriented society. The insatiability phenomenon that accompanies consumerism need not be a problem—it is simply regulated through marketlike arrangements, and citizens are relieved of the responsibility of considering whether certain types or levels of demand are inappropriate for the polity. It is in this sense that privatizing arrangements fail to enhance "public spirited action."

By contrast, Wildavsky argues that citizenship involves the changing or perfecting of preferences. Policy "changes may be judged better or worse by the degree to which they allow participants to learn whether what they once thought they wanted was what they now ought to have" (1979: 262). The last of the strategies for coping with demand overload, coproduction, holds some promise in this regard. Coproduction involves the sharing of responsibility for service delivery by citizens and government agents (Whitaker, 1980). The sharing can involve relatively complex arrangements, such as those that must be instituted for "coproducing" community safety through block watch and citizen crime patrol endeavors (Gluck, 1978); or the sharing can involve a very simple arrangement, such as that which obtains when curbside garbage collection replaces back-of-the-yard collection. In any case, coproduction involves the recognition that citizens can be producers as well as consumers of public services, at least in the sense that their inputs as "consumer producers" can supplement or substitute for some of the inputs of "professional producers" (Parks, et al., 1981).

The coproduction strategy is attractive because of its potential for enhancing the citizenship role while easing demand overload on government. As Levine (1984: 181) argues: "Coproduction lays the foundation for a positive relationship between government and citizens by making citizens an integral part of the service delivery process. Through these experiences citizens may build both competence and a broader perspective, a vision of the community and of what it can and should become" (1984: 181).

Coproduction is not without its problems, however. Coproduction might "co-opt" or divert citizen groups from advocating policy changes, provide urban officials with grounds for shifting blame about failure to deliver services, and ultimately "neutralize demands for policy change in service delivery" (Sharp, 1980b: 115). Coproduction may also run afoul of labor unions or professional groups that object to sharing their responsibilities with citizen volunteers; and both liability issues and civil service requirements can make it difficult for governments to set up coproduction arrangements (Bjur and Siegel, 1977). Finally, because advantaged citizens may be in a better position to engage in coproduction than are disadvantaged citizens, coproduction can have unwholesome consequences from the perspective of service equity (Rosentraub and Sharp, 1981).

Apart from coproduction, service rationing, and privatizing strategies, urban governments may attempt to deal with demand overload by finding ways of meeting demand that hide the nature and extent of government activity. That is, various strategies of "invisible government" (Aharoni, 1981) can be used to allocate services and benefits while shielding the public from information about who benefits, what amounts government is actually spending, and how much debt is actually being incurred. This response to demand overload does not reduce demand; but it provides government with greater maneuvering room to meet demand and to finance its endeavors without exciting the public's inclination to limit spending and debt.

James Bennett and Thomas DiLorenzo (1983), for example, document the growth of "off-budget enterprises" (OBEs) at the local level of government. OBEs, which include various districts, boards, authorities, commissions, and the like, are created by state and local governments for a variety of specific purposes, ranging from airport expansion to industrial development. These entities can issue bonds without concern about the legal restrictions on public debt that limit state and local governments, and they often have much more flexibility with respect to personnel and budgeting matters than do formal government agencies (Doig, 1983). From Bennett and DiLorenzo's perspective, what is significant about OBEs is that "an essential feature of all these organizations is that their financial activities do not appear in the budget of the government unit or units that created them. Thus, politicians have been able to make part of the public sector simply disappear by forming separate entities . . . to conduct borrowing and spending activities" (1983: 34).

Aharoni (1981) documents a variety of other methods by which government makes itself invisible, ranging from contracting arrangements to tax expenditures. Many of these are used primarily by the federal government, although contracting is also part of the repertoire of local governments. Like the other methods, it can be a device for responding to special interest pressures without appearing to expand the scope of government activity.

Most critics of "underground" or "invisible" government find these methods offensive primarily because they interfere with accountability. Aharoni, for example, argues: "Invisibility also avoids accountability. . . . Invisibility means that the true costs, beneficiaries, and relationships between costs and the decisions leading to them are not immediately clear. . . . Hidden costs and revenues give rise to fewer protests, confrontations, and conflicts than do revenues and expenditures that are publicly recorded" (1981: 114).

From the perspective of urban political economy, these methods of underground government constitute a means for emphasizing the prevailing interest of capitalists in infrastructure improvements that will enhance commercial and industrial development. In fact, the greatest growth in OBEs at the state and local levels has been in industrial development agencies, and the use of tax-exempt industrial revenue bonds has escalated into a major form of "corporate welfare" (Bennett and DiLorenzo, 1983).

This criticism of "underground government" is not necessarily the most telling, however. After all, many of the infrastructure improvements that are made by OBEs in the name of industrial development are related to concerns that the mass public expresses through individualized complaint-making. Crumbling roads and bridges, flooding problems, and the like are symptoms of a decaying urban infrastructure that has many impacts on the public (Choate and Walter, 1981), and many citizen-initiated demands are linked to these problems. What may be more problematic about "underground government" is that invisible government action means that citizens lose information about the totality of demands upon government and the real costs of meeting these demands. This leads to more than diminished government accountability. It also means that citizens are less able to understand the full scope of government's activities and the relevance of their own preferences and demands to the "invisible" component of government. If improvements can be made to the infrastructure without apparent cost to anyone and if many other projects are pursued without apparent implications for local governance, there is no reason for citizens to balance their demands for neighborhood-specific services against these competing needs. In short, invisible government, like privatization, can interfere with the citizenship role.

Conclusion

This chapter argues that urban governments, like national governments in postindustrial societies, may be experiencing demand overload. There are different components to the demand facing urban governments. Citizen-initiated contacting represents a method by which the mass public can directly register demands, frequently for basic housekeeping and problem-solving services in the neighborhood. In addition, urban governments in capitalist society can be said to face structural demand for projects and services that underwrite private sector activity.

With respect to the latter, overload in the form of fiscal crisis occurs because urban governments cannot adequately recoup the costs they must bear in underwriting private capital accumulation. With respect to the former, demand escalates as citizens' expectations grow; and the latter are fueled by the rhetoric and institutional arrangements of professionalized urban service bureaucracies and by the prevailing logic of "consumer" society.

The various strategies that urban governments use to respond to demand overload may be adaptive in the short run and from a narrow perspective; but in the longer run, or from a broader perspective, many of these strategies have counterproductive consequences. Privatizing strategies may introduce efficiencies and relieve government from direct responsibility for some services; but privatization provides further legitimacy for the erosion of the citizenship role into a consumer role. Strategies for hiding the true scope and cost of government activity have similar negative consequences for citizenship, and they interfere with accountability as well. Certain methods for rationing services can either block accountability or fuel citizen alienation. Coproduction appears most promising with respect to accountability and the citizenship role, but it may be difficult to orchestrate and has potential drawbacks of its own.

What is called for is undoubtedly some mix of these strategies, coupled with efforts to maximize the strengths and minimize the drawbacks of each. Stated another way, overloaded urban governments need public sector leaders who can respond to legitimate demands in suitable ways, say no to demands that are not in the public interest, provide means for citizens to appreciate the distinction, and ensure that there are mechanisms for recognizing and correcting the errors that government will inevitably make in judging which demands are in the public interest. These are admittedly heavy responsibilities for urban leaders; but the viability of cities in an era of demand overload surely hinges on the extent to which such leadership is forthcoming.

Appendix: Citizen Survey Methodology

The sampling frame for each of the 24 study neighborhoods consisted of all noncommercial telephone numbers listed for the areas as determined by geo-coding the Polk city directory. For each neighborhood, 300 phone listings were randomly drawn to achieve a goal of about 100 completed interviews per neighborhood. A matrix for random selection within the household (keyed to the number in the household over age 18) was used to select respondents. Those who had lived in the neighborhood for less than one year were screened out. At maximum, four callbacks per listing were attempted.

Students, a retired couple, and several middle-aged housewives served as paid interviewers. Training was provided by the principal investigator, and supervision was provided by the principal investigator and a graduate research assistant. The survey was conducted in the fall and winter months of 1982 and 1983. One of the two Spanish-fluent interviewers translated the interview schedule, and most of the interviews for the predominantly Hispanic neighborhood in the study were conducted in Spanish by these interviewers.

Between 73 and 100 usable interviews were generated for each neighborhood, for a total N of 2160. The overall completion rate for the survey is 64 percent. While this rate is well within the expected range for telephone surveys of the general population, some neighborhoods generated higher and some lower completion rates (lowest = 50 percent; highest = 78 percent). Neighborhood response rates were correlated with a variety of neighborhood characteristics. The only significant associations are a negative association with owner-occupied housing value and a positive association with percent black. In short, response rates were actually better in less-well-off neighborhoods and in neighborhoods with greater black population.

A copy of the screening sheet and interview schedule follows.

Appendix

Serial #

Col-Card:umn

1:1-4

TELEPHONE SCREEN

Hello, my name is _____ and I work for the Center for Public Affairs at the University of Kansas. We are taking a survey of the kinds of problems people have in their neighborhoods and how they get help from city government. Your phone number was selected at random for the survey, and we would appreciate your help.

Have you lived in Kansas City for a year or more?
(IF "NO" POLITELY TERMINATE INTERVIEW AND CODE RESULT NUMBER 12 ON THE RECORD OF CALL ATTEMPTS)

And have your lived in this general neighborhood for at least a year?
(IF "NO" POLITELY TERMINATE INTERVIEW AND CODE RESULT NUMBER 13 ON THE RECORD OF CALL ATTEMPTS)

Now I need to determine who in your household I should interview. Could you help me out by telling me just the first names of persons 18 years of age or older living at this residence? I only need the names of persons who, like yourself, have been here for at least one year. Please give the names in descending order of age. (IF PERSON ANSWERING PHONE IS THE ONLY ONE LIVING AT THE RESIDENCE, PROCEED TO INTERVIEW: OTHERWISE, ENTER NAMES ON THE DOTTED LINES 1-8 BELOW AND USE SELECTION MATRIX ON THE LABEL TO DETERMINE WHO TO INTERVIEW: ASK FOR THAT PERSON OR ARRANGE A CALLBACK)

1...................Oldest resident   5..................... 5th oldest
2...................2nd oldest   6..................... 6th oldest
3...................3rd oldest   7..................... 7th oldest
4...................4th oldest   8..................... 8th oldest

RECORD OF CONTACT ATTEMPTS

Date	Day of Week	Your ID	Result	Comments

RESULT CODES:
01-No answer
02-Not available
03-Line busy
04-Answer service
05-Lang. barrier
06-Callback set
07-Not in service
08-Non-residence
09-Completed
10-Refused
12-KC less than yr.
13-Nhbd. less than yr.

COMPLETION RECORD

Interviewer
ID # __ __   1:5-6

Date Completed
___/___ ___   1:7-10
  Month Day

Length of Interview
__ __   1:11-12
Minutes

Number in Household
(over age 18; see above)
__   1:13

CITIZEN SURVEY: KANSAS CITY CITIZEN CONTACTING STUDY

(READ BRACKETED SECTION ONLY IF RESPONDENT IS SOMEONE OTHER THAN
THE PERSON WHO FIRST ANSWERED THE PHONE)

[Hello, my name is _____. I'm working for a research project at the Center for Public Affairs at the University of Kansas. As part of our research, we are taking a survey of citizens in various Kansas City neighborhoods. We are studying the kinds of problems people have in their neighborhoods and how city government might deal with those problems. Your telephone number was selected at random for this survey.]
Though voluntary, your responses will help provide answers to important questions for Kansas City and other communities. Your responses are anonymous and will be kept confidential. We would appreciate your giving us about 15 minutes of your time for this survey.

(NOTE TIME OF BEGINNING INTERVIEW HERE) ___:___ am/pm

First of all, we are interested in what kinds of problems citizens of Kansas City may have in their neighborhoods.

1. What do you think is the most important problem that you have in your neighborhood?

                (DO NOT READ)   1( ) Problem mentioned
                                    2( ) No problem given
                                    3( ) Refusal

1:14

(WRITE IN BELOW WHAT THE PERSON SAID THE PROBLEM WAS. IF NO PROBLEM OR REFUSAL, SKIP TO ITEM #5)

_____
_____

2. How did this problem come about?

                           1( ) Gov't action/inaction
                           2( ) Citizen action/inaction
                           3( ) Nongov't. institution
                           4( ) Social force/condition
        (DO NOT READ)   5( ) Don't know
                           6( ) Refusal

1:15

3. How could the problem be solved?

                           1( ) Gov't action/inaction
                           2( ) Citizen action/inaction
                           3( ) Nongov't. institution
                           4( ) Social force/condition
        (DO NOT READ)   5( ) Don't know
                           6( ) Refusal

1:16

4. Do you think you could do something to help solve the problem.

                           1( ) Yes
                           2( ) Maybe
                           3( ) No
        (DO NOT READ)   4( ) Don't know
                           5( ) Refusal

1:17

Appendix

Now I will read a list of possible problems. Could you tell me whether each one is a big problem, somewhat of a problem, or not a problem at all in your neighborhood.

5. How about not having a park that is enjoyable? Is that...
   - 1( ) A big problem
   - 2( ) Somewhat of a problem
   - 3( ) Not a problem at all
   - (DO NOT READ) 4( ) Don't know
   - 5( ) Refused

   1:18

6. What about flooding when it storms?
   - 1( ) A big problem
   - 2( ) Somewhat of a problem
   - 3( ) Not a problem at all
   - (DO NOT READ) 4( ) Don't know
   - 5( ) Refused

   1:19

7. Houses that are rundown?
   - 1( ) A big problem
   - 2( ) Somewhat of a problem
   - 3( ) Not a problem at all
   - (DO NOT READ) 4( ) Don't know
   - 5( ) Refused

   1:20

8. Potholes or streets in bad repair?
   - 1( ) A big problem
   - 2( ) Somewhat of a problem
   - 3( ) Not a problem at all
   - (DO NOT READ) 4( ) Don't know
   - 5( ) Refused

   1:21

9. Not getting garbage picked up right?
   - 1( ) A big problem
   - 2( ) Somewhat of a problem
   - 3( ) Not a problem at all
   - (DO NOT READ) 4( ) Don't know
   - 5( ) Refused

   1:22

10. Houses that are not built to be safe?
    - 1( ) A big problem
    - 2( ) Somewhat of a problem
    - 3( ) Not a problem at all
    - (DO NOT READ) 4( ) Don't know
    - 5( ) Refused

    1:23

11. Mosquitos, rats or similar pests?
    - 1( ) A big problem
    - 2( ) Somewhat of a problem
    - 3( ) Not a problem at all
    - (DO NOT READ) 4( ) Don't know
    - 5( ) Refused

    1:24

12. Inadequate stop signs, traffic lights, or other traffic problems?
    - 1( ) A big problem
    - 2( ) Somewhat of a problem
    - 3( ) Not a problem at all
    - (DO NOT READ) ⌈ 4( ) Don't know
    - ⌊ 5( ) Refused

    1:25

13. Trash piles, junk or weeds on people's property?
    - 1( ) A big problem
    - 2( ) Somewhat of a problem
    - 3( ) Not a problem at all
    - (DO NOT READ) ⌈ 4( ) Don't know
    - ⌊ 5( ) Refused

    1:26

14. Vacant buildings that are dangerous?
    - 1( ) A big problem
    - 2( ) Somewhat of a problem
    - 3( ) Not a problem at all
    - (DO NOT READ) ⌈ 4( ) Don't know
    - ⌊ 5( ) Refused

    1:27

15. Streets not lighted well enough?
    - 1( ) A big problem
    - 2( ) Somewhat of a problem
    - 3( ) Not a problem at all
    - (DO NOT READ) ⌈ 4( ) Don't know
    - ⌊ 5( ) Refused

    1:28

16. Stray dogs or other animal problems?
    - 1( ) A big problem
    - 2( ) Somewhat of a problem
    - 3( ) Not a problem at all
    - (DO NOT READ) ⌈ 4( ) Don't know
    - ⌊ 5( ) Refused

    1:29

17. Poor bus service?
    - 1( ) A big problem
    - 2( ) Somewhat of a problem
    - 3( ) Not a problem at all
    - (DO NOT READ) ⌈ 4( ) Don't know
    - ⌊ 5( ) Refused

    1:30

18. Weeds or high grass?
    - 1( ) A big problem
    - 2( ) Somewhat of a problem
    - 3( ) Not a problem at all
    - (DO NOT READ) ⌈ 4( ) Don't know
    - ⌊ 5( ) Refused

    1:31

Now we have some questions about whether or not city government should be responsible for certain things. Do you think city government should:

19. Provide parks for the recreation and enjoyment of citizens?
    - 1( ) Yes
    - 2( ) No
    - (DO NOT READ) ⌈ 3( ) Don't know
    - ⌊ 4( ) Refused

    1:32

Appendix

20. Is it the city's responsibility to prevent storm water from flooding?
    - 1( ) Yes
    - 2( ) No
    - (DO NOT READ) ⎡3( ) Don't know
    - ⎣4( ) Refused

    1:33

21. Help citizens with repair of run-down housing?
    - 1( ) Yes
    - 2( ) No
    - (DO NOT READ) ⎡3( ) Don't know
    - ⎣4( ) Refused

    1:34

22. How about keeping streets repaird and free of potholes?
    - 1( ) Yes
    - 2( ) No
    - (DO NOT READ) ⎡3( ) Don't know
    - ⎣4( ) Refused

    1:35

23. Provide garbage collection service?
    - 1( ) Yes
    - 2( ) No
    - (DO NOT READ) ⎡3( ) Don't know
    - ⎣4( ) Refused

    1:36

24. Set and enforce standards on how homes should be built?
    - 1( ) Yes
    - 2( ) No
    - (DO NOT READ) ⎡3( ) Don't know
    - ⎣4( ) Refused

    1:37

25. Get rid of mosquitos, rats, and other health hazards?
    - 1( ) Yes
    - 2( ) No
    - (DO NOT READ) ⎡3( ) Don't know
    - ⎣4( ) Refused

    1:38

26. Make sure there are stop signs, traffic lights, and adequate traffic control?
    - 1( ) Yes
    - 2( ) No
    - (DO NOT READ) ⎡3( ) Don't know
    - ⎣4( ) Refused

    1:39

27. Make sure citizens do not have trash piles, junk, weeds or other problems on their property?
    - 1( ) Yes
    - 2( ) No
    - (DO NOT READ) ⎡3( )'Don't know
    - ⎣4( ) Refused

    1:40

28. Demolish dangerous vacant buildings if no better way can be found to make them safe?
    - 1( ) Yes
    - 2( ) No
    - (DO NOT READ) ⎡3( ) Don't know
    - ⎣4( ) **Refused**

    1:41

29. Insure that streets are adequately lighted at night?
    - 1( ) Yes
    - 2( ) No
    - (DO NOT READ) ⌈3( ) Don't know
    - ⌊4( ) Refused

    1:42

30. Make sure that stray dogs and other animal problems are taken care of?
    - 1( ) Yes
    - 2( ) No
    - (DO NOT READ) ⌈3( ) Don't know
    - ⌊4( ) Refused

    1:43

31. Provide bus service?
    - 1( ) Yes
    - 2( ) No
    - (DO NOT READ) ⌈3( ) Don't know
    - ⌊4( ) Refused

    1:44

32. Cut weeds and high grass on city land?
    - 1( ) Yes
    - 2( ) No
    - (DO NOT READ) ⌈3( ) Don't know
    - ⌊4( ) Refused

    1:45

33. In the past year, have you contacted any city government official or agency about any local problem or issue?
    - 1( ) Yes
    - 2( ) No
    - (DO NOT READ) ⌈3( ) Don't know
    - ⌊4( ) Refused

    1:46

    IF YES, CONTINUE   IF NO, DK, OR REFUSED, SKIP TO ITEM #45

34. How many different times did you make such a contact?
    (IF RESPONDENT UNSURE OF EXACT NUMBER, ASK "ABOUT HOW MANY")
    - 1( ) One   4( ) Four   7( ) More than 6
    - 2( ) Two   5( ) Five   8( ) Don't know
    - 3( ) Three 6( ) Six   9( ) Refused

    1:47

    (IF ANSWER TO #34 IS MORE THAN ONE, ASK THE FOLLOWING. IF NOT, SKIP TO ITEM #36)

35. Were any of these contacts repeated ones about the same problem?
    - 1( ) Yes
    - 2( ) No
    - (DO NOT READ) ⌈3( ) Don't know
    - ⌊4( ) Refused

    1:48

36. What was the contact about?
    - 1( ) Reason for contact given (WRITE IT IN BELOW)
    - (DO NOT READ) ⌈3( ) Don't know
    - ⌊4( ) Refused

    1:49

    _____
    _____
    _____

Appendix

37. With regard to your contact (MOST RECENT IF MORE THAN ONE) what was the main thing you wanted?
    (READ RESPONSES)
    - 1( ) Request a service
    - 2( ) Make a complaint about city service
    - 3( ) Ask for information
    - 4( ) Give an opinion on an issue

    (DO NOT READ)
    - 5( ) Don't know
    - 6( ) Refused

    1:50

38. Was the contact about something concerning you and your household, or something of concern for the community generally?
    - 1( ) Self/Household
    - 2( ) Community

    (DO NOT READ)
    - 3( ) Don't know
    - 4( ) Refused

    1:51

39. Who did you contact initially?
    (DO NOT READ RESPONSES UNLESS RESPONDENT GIVES YOU A NAME THAT YOU CAN'T CODE. IF SO, ASK RESPONDENT "IS THAT...?" AND READ LIST)
    - 01( ) "city hall"
    - 02( ) Action Center
    - 03( ) City Manager or Asst.
    - 04( ) Mayor
    - 05( ) City council member
    - 06( ) Public Information
    - 07( ) City attorney
    - 08( ) Specific city department (WRITE IT HERE: _____)
    - 09( ) Neighborhood leader
    - 10( ) Newspaper, TV, radio
    - 11( ) State or Federal agency or official
    - 12( ) Unable to code; respondent said: _____
    - 13( ) Don't know
    - 14( ) Refused

    1:52-53

40. How would you rate the promptness of the person or agency in dealing with your complaint or request? (READ RESPONSES)
    - 1( ) Excellent
    - 2( ) Good
    - 3( ) Acceptable
    - 4( ) Poor
    - 5( ) Unacceptable

    (DO NOT READ)
    - 6( ) Don't know
    - 7( ) Refused

    1:54

41. How good was the person or agency about doing what needed to be done about your request or complaint?

    (READ)
- 1( ) Excellent
- 2( ) Good
- 3( ) Acceptable
- 4( ) Poor
- 5( ) Unacceptable

    (DO NOT READ)
- 6( ) Don't know
- 7( ) Refused

1:55

42. How would you rate the courtesy of the person that you contacted?

    (READ)
- 1( ) Excellent
- 2( ) Good
- 3( ) Acceptable
- 4( ) Poor
- 5( ) Unacceptable

    (DO NOT READ)
- 6( ) Don't know
- 7( ) Refused

1:56

43. If you had a similar problem in the future, would you contact a city official or agency?

- 1( ) Yes
- 2( ) No

    (DO NOT READ)
- 3( ) Don't know
- 4( ) Refused

1:57

44. Who would you contact?

    (DO NOT READ RESPONSES)
- 01( ) "city hall"
- 02( ) Action Center
- 03( ) City Manager or Asst.
- 04( ) Mayor
- 05( ) City council member
- 06( ) Public Information
- 07( ) City attorney
- 08( ) Specific city department (WRITE IT HERE: _____)
- 09( ) Neighborhood leader
- 10( ) Newspaper, TV, radio
- 11( ) State or Federal agency or official
- 12( ) Unable to code; respondent said: _____
- 13( ) No one
- 14( ) Don't know
- 15( ) Refused

1:58-59

45. Have you had any problem that you did not contact the city about, even though you thought the city had something to do with the problem?

- 1( ) Yes

    (SKIP TO ITEM #53)
- 2( ) No
- 3( ) Don't know
- 4( ) Refused

1:60

Appendix

46. What was that problem about?

    (DO NOT READ)
    - 1( ) Problem given (WRITE IT IN HERE: _____)
    - 2( ) Don't know
    - 3( ) Refused

    1:61

Which of the following reasons describes why you did not contact anyone in city government about it?

47. You didn't know who to contact?
    - 1( ) Yes
    - 2( ) No
    - (DO NOT READ) 3( ) Can't remember
    - 4( ) Refused

    1:62

48. You thought it would involve too much red tape?
    - 1( ) Yes
    - 2( ) No
    - (DO NOT READ) 3( ) Can't remember
    - 4( ) Refused

    1:63

49. You thought it wouldn't do any good because city government isn't helpful?
    - 1( ) Yes
    - 2( ) No
    - (DO NOT READ) 3( ) Can't remember
    - 4( ) Refused

    1:64

50. You thought the problem wasn't important enough to bother?
    - 1( ) Yes
    - 2( ) No
    - (DO NOT READ) 3( ) Can't remember
    - 4( ) Refused

    1:65

51. You thought officials had been told already?
    - 1( ) Yes
    - 2( ) No
    - (DO NOT READ) 3( ) Can't remember
    - 4( ) Refused

    1:66

52. You just didn't have time to get involved or never got around to it?
    - 1( ) Yes
    - 2( ) No
    - (DO NOT READ) 3( ) Can't remember
    - 4( ) Refused

    1:67

53. Have you heard of the Action Center in Kansas City?

                        1( ) Yes
                        2( ) No
       (DO NOT READ) 3( ) Don't Know
                        4( ) Refused

1:68

(IF YES, CONTINUE)   (IF NO, DK, OR REFUSED, SKIP TO #56)

54. How did you find out about the Action Center?

                01( ) Friends, neighbors
                02( ) Community or neighborhood organization
   (DO NOT READ) 03( ) Radio
                04( ) Television
                05( ) Newspaper
                06( ) Water bill insert
                07( ) Bus poster
                08( ) City council member
                09( ) Other government official
                10( ) Don't remember
                11( ) Refusal

1:69-70

55. From what you have heard, what is the Action Center? That is, what does it do?

                   1( ) Correct response
   (DO NOT READ) 2( ) No response
                   3( ) Incorrect response
                   4( ) Refused

1:71

56. This past August, there was an election in Kansas City. Did you vote in that election?

                   1( ) Yes
                   2( ) No
   (DO NOT READ) 3( ) Don't know
                   4( ) Refused

1:72

57. What about <u>local</u> elections generally--do you always vote in those, do you sometimes miss one, or do you rarely vote, or do you never vote?

                   1( ) Always vote
                   2( ) Sometimes miss one
                   3( ) Rarely vote
                   4( ) Never vote
   (DO NOT READ) 5( ) Don't know
                   6( ) Refused

1:73

58. In the past three or four years have you attended any political meetings, like fund raisers or rallies or meetings with candidates?

                   1( ) Yes
                   2( ) No
   (DO NOT READ) 3( ) Don't know
                   4( ) Refused

1:74

Appendix

59. How interested would you say you are in the operations of city government?

    (READ)
    - 1( ) Very interested
    - 2( ) Somewhat interested
    - 3( ) Not at all interested

    (DO NOT READ)
    - 4( ) Don't know
    - 5( ) Refused

    1:75

60. Are you a member of any group or organization in this community that works to solve community problems?

    - 1( ) Yes
    - 2( ) No

    (DO NOT READ)
    - 3( ) Don't know
    - 4( ) Refused

    1:76

    (IF YES, ASK #61)   (IF NO, DK, OR REFUSED, SKIP TO #62)

61. What group or organization is that?

    (WRITE IT HERE) _____

62. Have you ever worked with your neighbors or other people in this community to do something about a local problem?

    - 1( ) Yes
    - 2( ) No

    (DO NOT READ)
    - 3( ) Don't know
    - 4( ) Refused

    1:77

63. How would you rate the overall quality of your neighborhood?

    (READ)
    - 1( ) Excellent
    - 2( ) Good
    - 3( ) Fair
    - 4( ) Poor
    - 5( ) Very poor

    (DO NOT READ)
    - 6( ) Don't know
    - 7( ) Refused

    1:78

64. How would you rate the quality of housing in your neighborhood?

    (READ)
    - 1( ) Excellent
    - 2( ) Good
    - 3( ) Fair
    - 4( ) Poor
    - 5( ) Very poor

    (DO NOT READ)
    - 6( ) Don't know
    - 7( ) Refused

    1:79

    1 1:80
    2:1-4 (REPEAT SERIAL #)

65. How about the quality of police protection in your neighborhood? Is it...

    (READ)
    - 1( ) Excellent
    - 2( ) Good
    - 3( ) Fair
    - 4( ) Poor

    (DO NOT READ)
    - 5( ) Very poor
    - 6( ) Don't know
    - 7( ) Refused

    2:5

66. What about the quality of street maintenance?
       1( ) Excellent
       2( ) Good
       3( ) Fair
       4( ) Poor
       5( ) Very poor
   (DO NOT READ) ⎡ 6( ) Don't know
                 ⎣ 7( ) Refused

67. How about parks and recreation in your neighborhood? How would you rate that?
       1( ) Excellent
       2( ) Good
       3( ) Fair
       4( ) Poor
       5( ) Very poor
   (DO NOT READ) ⎡ 6( ) Don't know
                 ⎣ 7( ) Refused

68. What about garbage collection?
       1( ) Excellent
       2( ) Good
       3( ) Fair
       4( ) Poor
       5( ) Very poor
   (DO NOT READ) ⎡ 6( ) Don't know
                 ⎣ 7( ) Refused

69. What about snow removal service?
       1( ) Excellent
       2( ) Good
       3( ) Fair
       4( ) Poor
       5( ) Very poor
   (DO NOT READ) ⎡ 6( ) Don't know
                 ⎣ 7( ) Refused

70. Compared to other neighborhoods in Kansas City, do you believe the quality of city services in your neighborhood is:
   (READ) ⎡ 1( ) Better
          ⎢ 2( ) About the same
          ⎣ 3( ) Worse
   (DO NOT READ) ⎡ 4( ) Don't know
                 ⎣ 5( ) Refused

71. Do you have any plans to move out of this neighborhood in the next year or two? Will you...
       1( ) Definitely move
       2( ) Probably move
       3( ) Probably not move
       4( ) Definitely not move
   (DO NOT READ) ⎡ 5( ) Don't know
                 ⎣ 6( ) Refused

2:6

2:7

2:8

2:9

2:10

2:11

Appendix

(IF DEFINITELY OR PROBABLY WILL MOVE, ASK #72;
IF ANY OTHER RESPONSE TO THE ABOVE QUESTION, ASK #73)

72. How important, if at all, is the quality of government and its services in your thinking about moving? Is it...

    1( ) Very important
    2( ) Somewhat important
    3( ) Not at all important
    (DO NOT READ) [4( ) Don't know
                    5( ) Refused
    (SKIP TO ITEM # 74)

73. Would you like to move in the near future if you could?

    1( ) Yes
    2( ) No
    (DO NOT READ) [3( ) Don't know
                    4( ) Refused

74. Do you think that the Kansas City government tries to provide the kinds of services that people in your neighborhood want?

    1( ) Yes
    2( ) No
    (DO NOT READ) [3( ) Don't know
                    4( ) Refused

75. How responsive are government officials to your concerns? Are they...

    1( ) Very responsive
    2( ) Somewhat responsive
    3( ) Only slightly responsive
    4( ) Not at all responsive
    (DO NOT READ) [5( ) Don't know
                    6( ) Refused

We are interested in how well-known the community leaders are in Kansas City.

76. Could you tell us the name of a city council member for your district? (DO NOT READ RESPONSES)

    01( ) J. Harold Hamil   09( ) Charles Hazley
    02( ) Joe Serviss   10( ) Jerry Riffel
    03( ) Joanne Collins   11( ) Rev. Emanuel Cleaver
    04( ) Kay Waldo   12( ) Evert Asjes III
    05( ) Leon Brownfield   13( ) Other name given
    06( ) Victor Swyden   14( ) Claims to know but
    07( ) Ed Quick   can't name
    08( ) Robert Hernandez   15( ) Don't know
                                  16( ) Refused

77. Any other city council member? (DO NOT READ RESPONSES)

    01( ) J. Harold Hamil   09( ) Charles Hazley
    02( ) Joe Serviss   10( ) Jerry Riffel
    03( ) Joanne Collins   11( ) Rev. Emanuel Cleaver
    04( ) Kay Waldo   12( ) Evert Asjes III
    05( ) Leon Brownfield   13( ) Other name given
    06( ) Victor Swyden   14( ) Claims to know; no name
    07( ) Ed Quick   15( ) Don't know
    08( ) Robert Hernandez   16( ) Refused

78. The city manager of Kansas City? (DO NOT READ RESPONSES)

   1( ) Robert Kipp
   2( ) Other name
   3( ) Claims to know; can't name
   4( ) Don't know
   5( ) Refused

   2:20

79. The mayor of Kansas City? (DO NOT READ RESPONSES)

   1( ) Richard Berkley
   2( ) Other name
   3( ) Claims to know; can't name
   4( ) Don't know
   5( ) Refused

   2:21

Finally, we have some general background questions. Your answers will be useful for comparing different sorts of neighborhoods and to help us to make sure that our survey is representative of Kansas City as a whole.

80. Do you own the place you are living, or are you renting?

   1( ) Own (or are buying)
   2( ) Renting
   3( ) Staying with someone
   4( ) Institutional boarding
   5( ) Other
   6( ) Refused

   2:22

81. Is the place you live in a house, an apartment, a trailer, or some other kind of building?

   1( ) House   5( ) Rooming house; hotel
   2( ) Trailer   6( ) Nursing home; institution
   3( ) Condominium   7( ) Other
   4( ) Apartment   8( ) Refused

   2:23

82. How many years of schooling have you had? (CIRCLE APPROPRIATE NUMBER)

   01 02 03 04 05 06   07 08 09 10 11 12
   Grade/Grammar School   High School

   13 14 15 16   17 18 19 20 21   99   88
   College or   Graduate/Profes-   Don't   Refused
   Technical School   sional School   Know

   2:24-25

83. What is your race or ethnic background?

   1( ) White
   2( ) Black
   3( ) Chicano/Hispanic
   4( ) Native American
   5( ) Asian
   6( ) Other
   7( ) Refused

   2:26

Appendix

84. We only need to know your approximate total income for the year. Is it...

    01( ) Below $5,000
    02( ) Between five and 10 thousand
    03( ) Between ten and 15 thousand
    04( ) Between 15 and 20 thousand
    05( ) Between 20 and 25 thousand
    06( ) Between 25 and 30 thousand
    07( ) Between 30 and 35 thousand
    08( ) Between 35 and 40 thousand
    09( ) Between 40 and 45 thousand
    10( ) Between 45 and 50 thousand
    11( ) Between 50 and 55 thousand
    12( ) Between 55 and 75 thousand
    13( ) Over $75,000
    14( ) Don't know
    15( ) Refused

    2:27-28

85. What is your age? ___ ___   00( ) Refused
                       YEARS   01( ) Don't know

    2:29-30

86. Respondent's sex (ASK ONLY IF UNSURE FROM SOUND OF VOICE)

    1( ) Male
    2( ) Female
    3( ) Refused

    2:31

    2: 32

Thank you very much for your help.   NOTE TIME ENDING INTERVIEW ___:___ am/pm

RETURN TO COVER SHEET AND FILL OUT COMPLETION RECORD

References

Adrian, Charles, and Oliver Williams. 1963. *Four Cities: A Study in Comparative Policy Making*. Philadelphia: University of Pennsylvania Press.

Aharoni, Yair. 1981. *The No-Risk Society*. Chatham, N.J.: Chatham House.

Alford, Robert, and Eugene Lee. 1968. "Voting Turnout in American Cities." *American Political Science Review* 62:796–813.

Almond, Gabriel, and Sidney Verba. 1963. *The Civic Culture*. Boston: Little, Brown.

Azar, Edward. 1978. "An Early Warning Model of International Hostilities." In Hazli Choucri and Thomas Robinson, eds., *Forecasting in International Relations*, pp. 223–38. San Francisco: W. H. Freeman.

Bahl, Roy. 1984. *Financing State and Local Government in the 1980s*. New York: Oxford University Press.

Balch, George. 1974. "Multiple Indications in Survey Research: The Concept 'Sense of Political Efficacy.'" *Political Methodology* 1:1–43.

Banfield, Edward. 1961. *Political Influence*. New York: Free Press.

Bell, Daniel. 1975. "The Revolution of Rising Entitlements." *Fortune* (April):98–103, 182, 185.

Bell, Daniel, and Virginia Held. 1969. "The Community Revolution." *The Public Interest* 16 (Summer):142–77.

Benjamin, Roger. 1980. *The Limits of Politics*. Chicago: University of Chicago Press.

Bennett, James, and Thomas DiLorenzo. 1983. *Underground Government: The Off-Budget Public Sector*. Washington, D.C.: Cato Institute.

Bish, Robert. 1976. "Fiscal Equalization through Court Decisions: Policymaking without Evidence." In Elinor Ostrom, ed., *The Delivery of Urban Services: Outcomes of Change*, pp. 75–102. Beverly Hills: Sage.

Bish, Robert, and Vincent Ostrom. 1973. *Understanding Urban Government*. Washington, D.C.: American Enterprise Institute for Public Policy Research.

Bjur, Wesley, and Gilbert Siegel. 1977. "Voluntary Citizen Participation in Local Government: Quality, Cost, and Commitment." *Midwest Review of Public Administration* 11:135–50.

Bollens, John, and Henry Schmandt. 1970. *The Metropolis: Its People, Politics, and Economic Life.* 2d ed. New York: Harper & Row.

Boyte, Harry. 1980. *The Backyard Revolution.* Philadelphia: Temple University Press.

Brittan, Arthur. 1977. *The Privatised World.* Boston: Routledge & Kegan Paul.

Brody, Richard, and Paul Sniderman. 1977. "From Life Space to Polling Place: The Relevance of Personal Concerns for Voting Behavior." *British Journal of Political Science* 7:337–60.

Burchell, Robert, and David Listokin, eds. 1981. *Cities under Stress: The Fiscal Crisis of Urban America.* Piscataway, N.J.: Rutgers University Center for Urban Policy Research.

Campbell, Angus; Gerald Gurin; and Warren Miller. 1954. *The Voter Decides.* Evanston, Ill.: Row Peterson.

———. 1960. *The American Voter.* New York: Wiley.

Campbell, Angus; Phillip Converse; and Willard Rodgers. 1976. *The Quality of American Life.* New York: Russell Sage Foundation.

Cebula, Richard. 1974. "Local Government Policies and Migration." *Public Choice* 19:85–93.

Chao, Joseph, and Stephen M. Renas. 1976. "More on Welfare and Migration." *Review of Business and Economic Research* 12 (Fall):90–91.

Choate, Pat, and Susan Walker. 1981. *America in Ruins.* Durham: Duke University Press.

Clark, Terry, and Lorna Ferguson. 1983. *City Money.* New York: Columbia University Press.

Coleman, Richard, and Bernice Neugarten. 1971. *Social Status in the City.* San Francisco: Jossey-Bass.

Converse, Philip. 1964. "The Nature of Belief Systems in Mass Publics." In David Apter, ed., *Ideology and Discontent*, pp. 206–61. New York: Free Press.

Coulter, Philip. 1984. "Particularized Contactors: Isolated Parochials or Complete Political Activists?" Paper presented at the Annual Meeting of the Southern Political Science Association, Savannah, Georgia, November 1–3.

Dagger, Richard. 1981. "Metropolis, Memory, and Citizenship." *American Journal of Political Science* 25:715–37.

Doig, Jameson. 1983. "'If I See a Murderous Fellow Sharpening a

Knife Cleverly . . .': The Wilsonian Dichotomy and the Public Authority Tradition." *Public Administration Review* 43:292–304.

Eisinger, Peter. 1972. "The Pattern of Citizen Contacts with Urban Officials." In Harlan Hahn, ed., *People and Politics in Urban Society*, pp. 43–69. Beverly Hills: Sage.

Elder, Charles, and Roger Cobb. 1983. *The Political Uses of Symbols.* New York: Longman.

Fainstein, Norman, and Susan Fainstein. 1982. "Restoration and Struggle: Urban Policy and Social Forces." In Norman Fainstein and Susan Fainstein, eds., *Urban Policy under Capitalism.* Beverly Hills: Sage.

Fitzgerald, Michael, and Robert Durant. 1980. "Citizen Evaluations and Urban Management: Service Delivery in an Era of Protest." *Public Administration Review* 40:585–94.

Fowler, Floyd, Jr. 1974. *Citizen Attitudes toward Local Government, Services, and Taxes.* Cambridge, Mass.: Ballinger.

Frederickson, George. 1973. *Neighborhood Control in the 1970's.* New York: Chandler.

Fuchs, Victor. 1968. *The Service Economy.* New York: Columbia University Press.

Gamson, William. 1968. *Power and Discontent.* Homewood, Ill.: Dorsey.

Gellhorn, Walter. 1966. *When Americans Complain.* Cambridge, Mass.: Harvard University Press.

Glantz, Frederic. 1975. "The Determinants of the Intrametropolitan Migration of the Poor." *Annals of Regional Science* (March):25–39.

Gluck, Peter. 1978. "Citizen Participation in Urban Services: The Administration of a Community-Based Crime Prevention Program." *Journal of Voluntary Action Research* 7 (January–April):33–44.

Gottdiener, Mark. 1983. "Understanding Metropolitan Deconcentration: A Clash of Paradigms." *Social Science Quarterly* 64:227–46.

Greene, Kenneth. 1982. "Administrators' Reactions to Elected Officials' Contacts: Avoidance or Cooperation." Paper presented at the Annual Meeting of the Southwestern Political Science Association, San Antonio, Texas, March 17–20.

Greenstein, J. David, and Paul Peterson. 1973. *Race and Authority in Urban Politics.* New York: Russell Sage Foundation.

Gutek, Barbara. 1978. "Strategies for Studying Client Satisfaction." *Journal of Social Issues* 34:44–56.

Hatry, Harry; Louis Blair; Donald Fisk; John Greiner; John Hall, Jr.; and Philip Schaenman. 1977. *How Effective Are Your Community Services?* Washington, D.C.: Urban Institute.

Hill, Richard C. 1978. "Fiscal Collapse and Political Struggle in Decaying Central Cities in the United States." In William K. Tabb and Larry Sawers, eds., *Marxism and the Metropolis*, pp. 213–400. New York: Oxford University Press.

Hirschman, Albert. 1970. *Exit, Voice, and Loyalty.* Cambridge, Mass.: Harvard University Press.

———. 1982. *Shifting Involvements.* Princeton: Princeton University Press.

Huckfeldt, R. Robert. 1979. "Political Participation and the Neighborhood Social Context." *American Journal of Political Science* 23:579–92.

Huntington, Samuel. 1975. "The Democratic Distemper." *Public Interest* 41 (Fall):9–38.

Ingram, Helen, and Dean Mann. 1980. "Policy Failure: An Issue Deserving Analysis." In Helen Ingram and Dean Mann, eds., *Why Policies Succeed or Fail*, pp. 11–32. Beverly Hills: Sage.

Jackson, John, ed. 1975. *Public Needs and Private Behavior in Metropolitan Areas.* Cambridge, Mass.: Ballinger.

Jones, Bryan. 1980. *Service Delivery in the City.* New York: Longman.

———. 1981. "Party and Bureaucracy: The Influence of Intermediary Groups on Urban Public Service Delivery." *American Political Science Review* 75:688–700.

Jones, Bryan; Saadia Greenberg; Clifford Kaufman; and Joseph Drew. 1977. "Bureaucratic Response to Citizen Initiated Contacts: Environmental Enforcement in Detroit." *American Political Science Review* 72:148–65.

Jones, Bryan, et al. 1978. "Service Delivery Rules and the Distribution of Local Government Services: Three Detroit Bureaucracies." *Journal of Politics* 40:332–68.

Kamer, Pearl. 1983. *Crisis in Urban Public Finance.* New York: Praeger.

Katznelson, Ira. 1981. *City Trenches.* Chicago: University of Chicago Press.

Keller, Suzanne. 1968. *The Urban Neighborhood; A Sociological Perspective.* New York: Random House.

Kennedy, Michael. 1984. "The Fiscal Crisis of the City." In M. P.

Smith, ed., *Cities in Transformation*, pp. 91–110. Beverly Hills: Sage.

King, Leslie, and Reginald Golledge. 1978. *Cities, Space and Behavior: The Elements of Urban Geography*. Englewood Cliffs, N.J.: Prentice-Hall.

Lasswell, Harold. 1936. *Politics: Who Gets What, When, How*. New York: McGraw-Hill.

Lazarsfeld, Paul; Bernard Berelson; and Hazel Gaudet. 1948. *The People's Choice*. New York: Columbia University Press.

Levine, Charles. 1984. "Citizenship and Service Delivery: The Promise of Coproduction." *Public Administration Review* 44:178–86.

Levy, Frank; Arnold Meltsner; and Aaron Wildavsky. 1974. *Urban Outcomes*. Berkeley and Los Angeles: University of California Press.

Lineberry, Robert. 1977. *Equality and Urban Policy*. Beverly Hills: Sage.

Lipsky, Michael. 1980. *Street-Level Bureaucracy*. New York: Russell Sage Foundation.

Lipsky, Michael, and Margaret Levi. 1972. "Community Organization as a Political Resource." in Harlan Hahn, ed., *People and Politics in Urban Society*, pp. 175–99. Beverly Hills: Sage.

Long, Norton. 1972. *The Unwalled City*. New York: Basic Books.

Lovrich, Nicholas. 1974. "Differing Priorities in an Urban Electorate: Service Preferences among Anglo, Black and Mexican-American Voters." *Social Science Quarterly* 55:704–17.

Maslow, Abraham. 1948. "'Higher' and 'Lower' Needs." *Journal of Psychology* 25:433–36.

Meyerson, Martin, and Edward Banfield. 1955. *Politics, Planning, and the Public Interest*. New York: Free Press.

Milward, H. Brinton. 1980. "Policy Entrepreneurship and Bureaucratic Demand Creation." In Helen Ingram and Dean Mann, eds., *Why Policies Succeed or Fail*, pp. 255–77. Beverly Hills: Sage.

Mladenka, Kenneth. 1978. "Citizen Demand and Bureaucratic Response: Direct Dialing Democracy in a Major American City." In Robert Lineberry, ed., *The Politics and Economics of Urban Services*, pp. 11–28. Beverly Hills: Sage.

Nathan, Richard, and Charles Adams. 1976. "Understanding Central City Hardship." *Political Science Quarterly* 91:47–62.

Neal, Arthur, and Melvin Seeman. 1964. "Organizations and Powerlessness: A Test of the Mediation Hypothesis." *American Sociological Review* 29:216–26.

References

Neiman, Max. 1982. "An Exploration into Class Clustering and Local-Government Inequality." In Richard Rich, ed., *Analyzing Urban-Service Distributions*, pp. 219–33. Lexington, Mass.: Lexington Books.

Nie, Norman; G. Bingham Powell; and Kenneth Prewitt. 1969. "Social Structure and Political Participation: Developmental Relationships." *American Political Science Review* 63:808–32.

Niskanen, W. A. 1971. *Bureaucracy and Representative Government*. Chicago; Aldine-Atherton.

O'Brien, David. 1975. *Neighborhood Organization and Interest-Group Processes*. Princeton: Princeton University Press.

O'Connor, James. 1973. *The Fiscal Crisis of the State*. New York: St. Martin's Press.

Orbell, John, and Toru Uno. 1972. "A Theory of Neighborhood Problem Solving: Political Action vs. Residential Mobility." *American Political Science Review* 66:471–89.

Ostrom, Elinor. 1976. *The Delivery of Urban Services*. Beverly Hills: Sage.

Pack, Janet. 1973. "Determinants of Migration to Central Cities." *Journal of Regional Science* 13:249–60.

Parks, Roger; Paula Baker; Larry Kiser; Ronald Oakerson; Elinor Ostrom; Vincent Ostrom; Stephen Percy; Martha Vandivort; Gordon Whitaker; and Rick Wilson. 1981. "Consumers as Producers of Public Services: Some Economic and Institutional Considerations." *Policy Studies Journal* 9 (Summer):1001–10.

Peterson, Paul. 1981. *City Limits*. Chicago: University of Chicago Press.

Quigley, John. 1980. "Local Residential Mobility and Local Government Policy." In W. A. V. Clark and Eric Moore, eds., *Residential Mobility and Public Policy*. Beverly Hills: Sage.

Reissman, Leonard. 1970. *The Urban Process*. New York: Free Press.

Rich, Richard. 1982a. "The Political Economy of Urban-Service Distribution." In Richard Rich, ed., *The Politics of Urban Public Services*, pp. 1–16. Lexington, Mass.: D. C. Heath.

———. 1982b. *Analyzing Urban-Service Distributions*. Lexington, Mass.: D. C. Heath.

———. 1982c. "The Political Economy of Public Services." In Norman Fainstein and Susan Fainstein, eds., *Urban Policy under Capitalism*, pp. 191–212. Beverly Hills: Sage.

Rosentraub, Mark, and Elaine Sharp. 1981. "Consumers as Producers of Social Services: Coproduction and the Level of Social Services." *Southern Review of Public Administration* 4:502–39.

Rubin, Irene. 1982. *Running in the Red: The Political Dynamics of Urban Fiscal Stress.* Albany: State University of New York Press.

Savas, E. S. 1982. *Privatizing the Public Sector.* Chatham, N.J.: Chatham House.

Schlozman, Kay, and Sidney Verba. 1979. *Injury to Insult.* Cambridge, Mass.: Harvard University Press.

Schneider, Mark, and John Logan. 1982. "The Effects of Local Government Finances on Community Growth Rates: A Test of the Tiebout Model." *Urban Affairs Quarterly* 18:91–105.

Seligson, Mitchell. 1980. "A Problem-Solving Approach to Measuring Political Efficacy." *Social Science Quarterly* 60:630–42.

Sharp, Elaine. 1980a. "Citizen Perceptions of Channels for Urban Service Advocacy: The Role of Citizen Organizations." *Public Opinion Quarterly* 33:362–76.

———. 1980b. "Toward a New Understanding of Urban Services and Participation: The Coproduction Concept." *Midwest Review of Public Administration* 14:105–18.

———. 1982. "Citizen-Initiated Contacting of Government Officials and Socioeconomic Status: Determining the Relationship and Accounting for It." *American Political Science Review* 76:109–15.

———. 1984a. "'Exit, Voice, and Loyalty' in the Context of Local Government Problems." *Western Political Quarterly* 37:67–83.

———. 1984b. "Need, Awareness, and Contacting Propensity: Study of a City with a Central Complaints Unit." *Urban Affairs Quarterly* 20:22–30.

———. 1984c. "Citizen Demand-Making in the Urban Context." *American Journal of Political Science* 28:654–70.

Simmons, J. W. 1968. "Changing Residence in the City: A Review of Intra-Urban Mobility." *Geographical Review* 58:622–51.

Smith, Michael. 1979. *The City and Social Theory.* New York: St. Martin's Press.

———. 1984. *Cities in Transformation: Class, Capital, and the State.* Beverly Hills: Sage.

Sniderman, Paul, and Richard Brody. 1977. "Coping: The Ethic of Self-Reliance." *American Journal of Political Science* 21:501–22.

Sniderman, Paul; Richard Brody; and James Kuklinski. 1984. "Policy Reasoning and Political Values: The Problem of Racial Equality." *American Journal of Political Science* 28:75–94.

Stanley, David T. 1980. "Cities in Trouble." In Charles Levine, ed.,

Managing Fiscal Stress, pp. 95–122. Chatham, N.J.: Chatham House.

Stipak, Brian. 1979. "Citizen Satisfaction with Urban Services: Potential Misuse as a Performance Indicator." *Public Administration Review* 39:46–52.

———. 1980. "Using Clients to Evaluate Programs." Paper presented at the Symposium on the Public Encounter, Virginia Polytechnic Institute and State University, Blacksburg, Virginia.

Thomas, John. 1982. "Citizen-Initiated Contacts with Government Agencies: A Test of Three Theories." *American Journal of Political Science* 26:504–22.

Thompson, Victor. 1975. *Without Sympathy or Enthusiasm*. University, Ala.: University of Alabama Press.

Tiebout, Charles. 1956. "A Pure Theory of Local Expenditures." *Journal of Political Economy* 64:416–24.

U.S. Bureau of the Census. 1982. *1982 Census of Governments*, Vol. 4, *Government Finances*, No. 4, *Finances of Municipal and Township Governments*. Washington, D.C.: U.S. Government Printing Office.

Vedlitz, Arnold; James Dyer; and Roger Durand. 1980. "Citizen Contacts with Local Governments: A Comparative View." *American Journal of Political Science* 24:50–67.

Vedlitz, Arnold, and Eric Veblen. 1980. "Voting and Contacting: Two Forms of Political Participation in a Suburban Community." *Urban Affairs Quarterly* 16:31–48.

Verba, Sidney, and Norman Nie. 1972. *Participation in America*. New York: Harper & Row.

Washnis, George. 1972. *Municipal Decentralization and Neighborhood Resources*. New York: Praeger.

Whitaker, Gordon. 1980. "Coproduction: Citizen Participation in Service Delivery." *Public Administration Review* 40:240–46.

Wildavsky, Aaron. 1979. *Speaking Truth to Power*. Boston: Little, Brown.

Yates, Douglas. 1977. *The Ungovernable City*. Cambridge, Mass.: MIT Press.

Index

Action Center, 19-21, 29, 87-100, 101n, 102-20, 123-25, 129-30, 168
Awareness, of government, 11-13, 40, 45-46, 48-49, 52-54, 57, 81, 84, 109-12, 129, 131n

Bureaucratic decision rules, 4, 117, 180

Campaign activity, 9-11, 44
Centralized complaint-handling units, 7, 13, 18-19, 21, 29, 45, 88, 102-103, 108-13, 117, 124, 129, 130-31n, 161. *See also* Ombudsman
Communal participation, 10, 33, 36, 43-44, 156-57
Community organization: involvement in, 9, 71, 74-77, 156-57. *See also* Neighborhood: organizations
Connoisseurship, 68-70, 73-75, 77
Consumerism, 173-76, 181
Contacting, citizen initiated: defined, 3-6; channels for, 102-103, 108, 112, 124; difficulty of, 9, 42; patterns of, 12-13, 21, 48-49, 52, 55, 60-61, 67, 110, 112, 128, 156-57; and neighborhood organizations, 17, 82-99; and centralized complaint-handling units, 18, 108-109; and political attitudes, 38-39; as instrumental behavior, 40, 58; compared with other behaviors, 43-44, 154, 169, 175; and perceived need, 51; and threshold levels, 54; in Dallas and Houston, 57, 108, 110; and neighborhood social context, 62
Coproduction, 179, 181-82, 185

Demand: creation by government, 69, 71-73, 75-76, 170, 172-73, 175; overload, 19, 162-66, 168-70, 175-82, 184-85
Demand-making, 2-3, 55-56, 59, 62, 65, 67, 77, 81-83, 89-92, 94, 96-100, 106-107, 113, 130, 133-34, 139-40, 161-62, 171, 174

Education, 15, 32, 37, 44, 48-52, 54-55, 58-61, 74, 77, 99, 103, 140
Efficacy, 8-9, 16, 38-42, 49, 54-55, 104, 130
Equity, 69
Exit: as response to discontent, 138-40, 143, 153-56, 161
Expectations of government, 67-77, 81, 100, 162-65, 169-70, 172-78, 184

Fiscal stress. *See* Revenue, local government

General referent contacting, 10, 14, 32-37

Homeownership, 71, 74

Income, 15, 32, 37, 50-52, 59, 74, 77
Inequality, 73-76, 80, 136-37
Inequity, 73
Interest in government. *See* Political interest

Knowledge of government, 16, 38-42, 45-46, 48, 52, 84, 129-30, 131n

Loyalty: as a response to discontent, 139

Need, 11-13, 45-46, 48-49, 52-55, 57, 60-61, 70, 81, 84, 108-10, 113, 125, 128-29, 131n. *See also* Perceived need
Need-awareness model, 11-17, 39-40, 45-46, 48, 51-52, 54, 57, 67, 81-85, 92, 94, 100, 110, 128-29
Neighborhood: as level of analysis, 57-58; organizations, 17-18, 26-29, 58-59, 72, 76, 83, 89-100, 106-107, 129-30, 169, 175

Objective conditions, 17, 46, 59, 62-63, 65, 67-70, 72-73, 75, 78, 80-81, 100; as rated by trained observers, 63-64

210

Index

Objective need, 17, 46, 58, 64–68, 71, 74–77, 79–80, 100, 129–30
Off-budget enterprises, 182–83
Ombudsman, 5, 7–8, 124

Particularized contacting, 10–11, 14, 32–37, 43
Perceived need, 15, 17–18, 46, 49–52, 54, 58, 62–63, 65, 67–68, 70–77, 79–81, 84, 94, 100, 110, 129
Policy complexity, 170–72
Political economy, 176–78
Political interest, 15–16, 38–42, 72, 74, 129–30
Positive bias: in citizen evaluations, 78–80, 100
Privatization, 179–82, 185

Quality of life, 62–64, 68, 77, 80

Race, 15, 32, 103–104
Rationing of services, 179, 182, 185
Reform, 6, 19, 22, 42, 116, 124, 172, 175
Residential mobility, 59, 62, 133–55, 158–61
Responsiveness of government, 18, 119–25, 131n, 133, 159–61
Revenue, local government, 165–67

Satisfaction: with government response, 113–15, 117, 119–25, 158
Self-reliance, ethic of, 18, 164–65
Service delivery, 1–3, 23, 55, 76, 80, 107, 116, 133–35, 139–44, 149–54, 160, 162, 169–72, 174, 178, 181–82
Social context: in neighborhood, 17, 57–58, 60, 62, 81, 130
Social status, 8, 59–60, 62, 70, 140. *See also* Social well-being
Social well-being, 12, 45–46, 49, 61, 108, 110–11, 125, 128–29
Socioeconomic model, 8–12, 14–18, 32–33, 37–40, 43, 46–48, 58–59, 62, 99–100, 128–29
Socioeconomic status, 12, 17, 37, 46, 48–51, 59, 69–70, 77, 130
Stakeholding, 69–76
Study neighborhoods, 24–27, 29, 63–64, 84

Thresholds, 48–49, 52–54, 84, 128

Urban services. *See* Service delivery

Voice: as a response to discontent, 18, 138–40, 143, 156–59, 161
Voting, 9–11, 42–44, 156–57

About the Author

Elaine B. Sharp teaches political science at the University of Kansas. She received her B.A. from Carlow College in Pittsburgh, her M.A. from the University of Illinois at Chicago Circle, and her Ph.D. from the University of North Carolina at Chapel Hill. This is her first book.